MW01620298

SACRED TREE
FOR ALL SEASONS

ALSO BY DANY LYNE

Riding the Wave:
Tales of Transformation
2014

ME TOO LOUD & CLEAR:
How I Walked the Talk from Silence to Active Hope
2019

Reiki Plus Plus:
Embrace Your Sacred Tree to Transcend Trauma
2019

SACRED TREE FOR ALL SEASONS

GUIDEBOOK TO RECLAIM YOUR CAPACITY TO HEAL

DANY LYNE

UNLEASH, TORONTO, CANADA

Lyne, Dany, 1962-, author
Sacred Tree For All Seasons: Guidebook To Reclaim Your Capacity To Heal / Dany Lyne.

ISBN: 978-0-9939204-3-1

Copy editing and proofreading: Strong Finish Editorial Design
Art direction: Dany Lyne
Design: Candice Craig at Alchemy Design & Andrea Gifford at agiff design
Photoshop art: Sharon Switzer
Illustrations: Dany Lyne

Printed and bound in Canada.

For those who embrace radical transformation
and Love as a new word, a new kind of open:

Rémy Huberdeau
Lou Jurgens
Helgi Maki

AUTHOR'S NOTE

The information provided in *Sacred Tree for All Seasons* is believed to be accurate and sound, based on my knowledge and experience. This book is a synthesis of my channelled insights, thoughts, opinions, and conclusions. How you decide to use the information I present is up to you. Using the techniques herein is acknowledging that you have read, understand, and agree to this disclaimer and therefore that informed consent has been established.

ACKNOWLEDGEMENTS

I thank Jessamyn Smith for introducing me to the medical Qigong and traditional Chinese medicine (TCM) body of knowledge encapsulated by the regenerative or creative cycle. The crumpled chart she referred to in my Reiki Workshops kicked off an extensive exploration of the wisdom chronicled by Chinese shamans and passed on to medical Qigong and TCM practitioners despite the Cultural Revolution. I am grateful for Donna Oliver's inspiring medical Qigong classes and her input in the early stages of this process. I also wish to recognize Scott Davis's insightful feedback just before I wrote the last draft. And most poignantly, I'm indebted to the many generous ancestral guides and spirit animals for downloading via my channel the less-documented ancient knowledge pertaining to the emotional, mental, and spiritual manifestation of the TCM regenerative cycle.

I am forever grateful to all the clients and students who invited me to join their healing and transformational journeys. Without their trust and generosity, I would not have had the honour of being a compassionate witness often enough to observe the magnificent competence of the human organism in self-healing action. The proficiency of their energy bodies (including their physical body) to transcend trauma (including sexual abuse trauma) speaks to the power and manifestation of innate harmony in action. Initially discovering, and later uncovering, their built-in high-frequency resources and self-healing capacity motivates me to share the enchanting magic of our innate alchemical vigour: our Sacred Tree in cyclical action.

I am grateful that Damian Rogers read the mega-manuscript I dropped off on her porch in the spring of 2018. Her perspicacity and enthusiasm in the early stages of what I refer to as "The Sacred Tree Trilogy" permeate all the content that under her guidance transformed into several books, including *Reiki Plus Plus: Embrace Your Sacred Tree to Transcend Trauma*. Last but not least, I am forever grateful for the production team's work, namely: Candice Craig's preliminary design, Andrea Gifford's expert complementary design and layout, Sharon Switzer's Photoshop magic, and Heather Sangster's hawk eye for details.

I am also indebted to Allyson Taché, the beautiful woman I was introduced to in a yoga class who, after spending two hours together in a coffee house reminiscing about our mutual journeys in Burkina Faso, offered me her loft in a secluded fifteenth-century tower in a small town in Corsica, France. The bulk of these manuscripts were channelled and chiselled on the rooftop of this ancient tower held tightly by the windswept mountains and Mediterranean Sea as well as the robust and magical Maquis shrubland of Le Cap Corse. I also thank Allyson and my beloved neighbours—Deirdre Newman, Roy Pelletier, and Evelyne Desutter—for their spirit, laughter, and joyful car rides into town for groceries and supplies, not to mention exquisite afternoons on the beach and on the trails. My spirit soared on their welcoming wings, and these pages are imbued with their generosity.

Thank you, Katherine Dynes, for being a stalwart ally and friend regardless of the velocity of my enthusiasm and tenacity when manifesting creative projects! Your generous and insightful input during all stages of development—including the writing process, design, and production—permeates this book. I also thank my limited market survey team, who helped me finalize the oracle card design: Ashley Overholt and Cynthia Hawkins.

CONTENTS

INTRODUCTION

RECLAIMING YOUR INNATE HEALING RESOURCES

Living fully and thriving hinges on your vibrant interconnection with your indispensable grounding cord to the centre of the earth and your simultaneous impulse to grow upward to the sun. This potent flow of healing energy is foundational and available to you regardless of the state you are in. Thankfully, an aspect of you is always inherently aligned with not only the sun and the earth but also the multidimensional and cyclical expressions of harmony, such as compassion, inner peace, trust, dignity, and wisdom. This fountainhead of high-vibration resources and ancient cyclical rhythms is the essence of your innate Sacred Tree.

All living beings share this orientation and progression, but trees, more than any other, palpably live these teachings and share them with us. This guidebook and the oracle cards are tools to help you align with the wisdom of trees and their flowing collaboration with the elemental Spirits of Wood, Fire, Earth, Metal, and Water. When you approach these cards in a contemplative state, they can transmit to you these Spirits' blessings and the medicine you need to tap into and activate the life-sustaining elemental resources of your Sacred Tree.

As you know, your human experience is never static. You are showered, or bombarded (depending on the day), with a perpetual flow of wholesome and unwholesome inputs. Therefore, you are always somewhere in the continuum between harmony and disharmony. Consequently, the harmony and health of your Sacred Tree ecology is synonymous with keeping your house in order—when you do not clean your house regularly, you soon dwell in a chaotic, congested, unproductive, and unpleasant environment. It's inescapable. The same patent wisdom applies to your Sacred Tree.

Although you may suffer from estrangement from trees and your Sacred Tree-ness, these oracle cards can help you re-establish a conscious and mindful interdependence with the elemental healing energies within yourself. Hence, their application extends far beyond that of a fortune cookie; they are power tools to reunite you with your elemental Spirits of Wood, Fire, Earth, Metal and Water—your innate high-vibration resources in your body. It is my hope that these oracle cards and the guidebook are for you what electricity and the advent of the washing machine was to your household!

This guidebook and the oracle cards are designed to help you change your life from the inside out! Pulling cards and doing readings: assists you in decoding the messages that your illnesses, dis-eases, and manifestations of disharmony are attempting to convey; demystifies the root causes of your dis-eases, illnesses, and/or malaise on the physical, emotional, mental, and/or spiritual levels; supports your self-inquiry and personal energetic work, such as self-Reiki, to create changes in all four energy fields (physical, emotional, mental, and spiritual), something that surgery, legal/illegal drugs, and many forms of talk therapy don't necessarily accomplish; and reconnects you with your innate self-healing resources—the elemental Spirits of Wood, Fire, Earth, Metal, and Water—no matter what hullaballoo is unfolding in your day-to-day life.

Have fun with it! The Spirits of Wood, Fire, Earth, Metal, and Water are delighted to be in conversation with you. Their purpose is to support you and shower you with their healing energy, wisdom, and blessings. Figuring out the ancient Chinese elemental system is not necessary—no effort is required beyond showing up. Let the cards do that work for you. Just set aside some time to pull some cards and open up to receive the elemental Spirits' messages.

THE DISHARMONY STORIES

If you're wondering what this or that disharmony looks like when it manifests in live Technicolor action, then this section is for you! As a spirit having a human experience, I also have the privilege of navigating harmony and disharmony in action; hence, the stories with clear autobiographical references depict people and events in my life. As a practitioner, I am honoured to witness the sacred journeys of many individuals in the context of sessions; hence, the other stories I share have revealed themselves during sessions with clients. Please note that to protect client privacy, their traits, events, and locations have often been shifted to equivalents. I am most grateful for the opportunity to share our stories to alleviate the fog between the precious dots of wisdom we need to connect in order to reactivate our magnificent Sacred Trees and transcend our limitations and trauma.

USING THE CARDS TO FOCUS YOUR SELF-REIKI AND REIKI PRACTICE

Many of you already use self-Reiki and Reiki, recognizing it as a merciful tool to soothe your discomfort and suffering. Unfortunately, whether a Reiki practitioner or not, many of my clients and students do not interact efficiently or distinctly with the physical, emotional, mental, and spiritual manifestations of harmony and disharmony. Hence, these oracle cards and the guidebook are learning tools as well. First, they inform your self-healing, self-Reiki, and Reiki practice enough to efficiently harness the manifestation of your magnificent high-vibration resources in these four energy bodies. Second, they energize and focus your meditative self-healing or healing practice enough to release "the stuckness" that is causing disharmony in these four energy bodies.

Moreover, many of my clients and students do not know where their organs sit in their body or how to efficiently reawaken the elemental wisdom and medicine in their organs. As the chakra system has exploded into popular culture via the widespread study and practice of yoga asanas, it has become the most common language used to describe the architecture of the energy body when teaching energy medicine modalities. Reiki practitioners, in particular, often focus on the chakra system as a tool for diagnosis and healing. Although it says a lot about a super beautiful and exciting shift in the dominant culture, this flood of information on the chakras has eclipsed the resources and brightness of your less glittery and more slithery healing allies: your yin and yang organs.

The use of the oracle cards—especially when coupled with radical self-inquiry, self-Reiki, and Reiki—can unleash enough energy and traction to uplift you or your clients beyond survival mode, support you in the ongoing exigencies of life and living well, and energize you or your clients' project evolution.

Let the self-healing begin!

CHAPTER ONE

YOUR SACRED TREE'S ELEMENTAL AND CYCLICAL WISDOM

ONLY READ THIS CHAPTER IF YOU'RE SUPER CURIOUS!

These teachings are built into the oracle cards and your readings regardless!

YOUR FIVE YIN–YANG ORGAN ALLIANCES

Your Sacred Tree ecology, alchemical fortitude, and resilience rests in the fact that you have a built-in self-healing system. Your Sacred Tree is equipped with five specialized energetic orbs, each including solid yin organs and hollow yang organs paired together in dynamic healing teams.

a. While your **yin organs** (namely the liver, heart, spleen/pancreas, lungs, and kidneys/brain/reproductive organs) do their extensively acknowledged biological work, they also work energetically on the physical, emotional, mental, and spiritual levels.

b. Your hollow **yang organs** are doing just as much physically and energetically. They process the food you eat, eliminate the unwholesome byproducts, and transform and later imbibe wholesome nutrients. They help absorb and integrate all the energy that is beneficial and nutritious and eliminate all the energy that is harmful and detrimental.

Although some of these alliances seem logical, some may surprise you, especially if allopathic medicine has been your dominant template for health and healing.

a. When you nurture and cleanse your gallbladder, you heal your liver. *Sure.*

b. When you nurture and cleanse your small intestine, you heal your heart. *What?*

c. When you nurture and cleanse your stomach, you heal your spleen and pancreas. *Okay.*

d. When you nurture and cleanse your colon, you heal your lungs. *What?*

e. When you nurture and cleanse your bladder, you heal your kidneys. *Sure.*

THE FIVE EXTERNAL ORGANS INCLUDED

This Chinese elemental system is vast. Your entire physical body, including all of its tissues, is mapped out on its grid. Although I decided to focus on the yin–yang internal organ groupings within each elemental orb, I discovered that if I also included the external sense organs, I opened up the template enough to uncover more clearly your mighty trauma healing matrix. These partnerships reveal very salient information about your experience and process in traumatic conditions and your corresponding capacity to heal. Therefore, each card description, whether harmony or disharmony, reveals the dynamic relationship between your:

a. eyes, sight, and the liver/gallbladder;

b. tongue, verbal expression, and the heart/duodenum/small intestine;

c. mouth, consumption, and spleen/pancreas/stomach;

d. nose, in-and-out exchange, and the lungs/colon; and

e. ears, hearing, and the kidneys/bladder.

GENERATING CYCLE

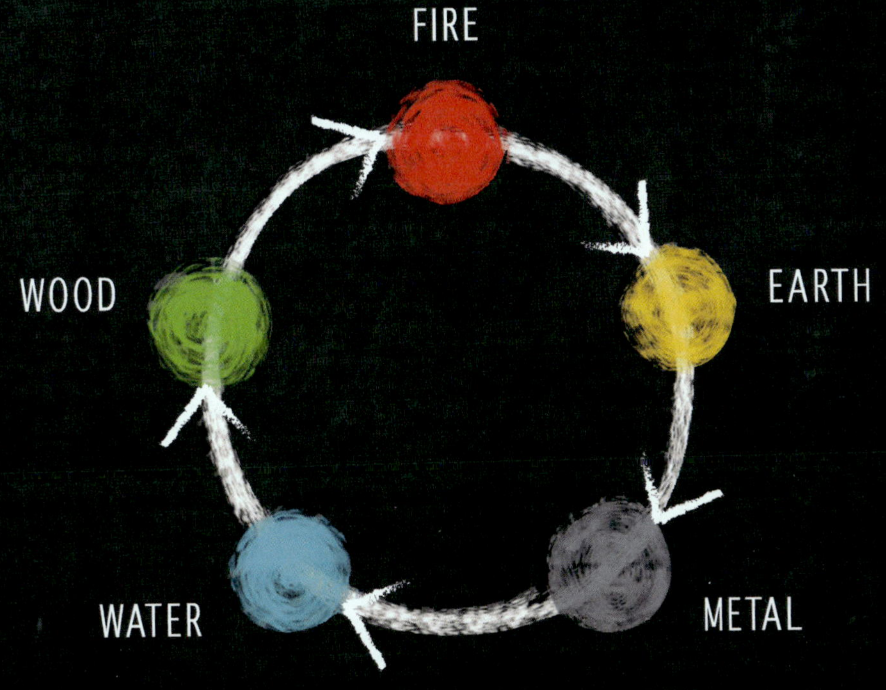

FIVE YIN–YANG ORGAN ALLIANCES

ELEMENTS	WOOD 木	FIRE 火	EARTH 土	METAL 金	WATER 水
SEASONS	Spring	Summer	Late Summer	Autumn	Winter
YIN ORGANS	Liver	Heart	Spleen Pancreas	Lungs	Kidneys Brain Reproductive Organs
YANG ORGANS	Gallbladder	Duodenum Small Intestine	Stomach	Colon	Bladder Sea of Marrow
EXTERNAL ORGANS	Eyes Third Eye	Tongue	Mouth	Nose	Ears

ORGANS AND THEIR ELEMENTAL ALLIANCES

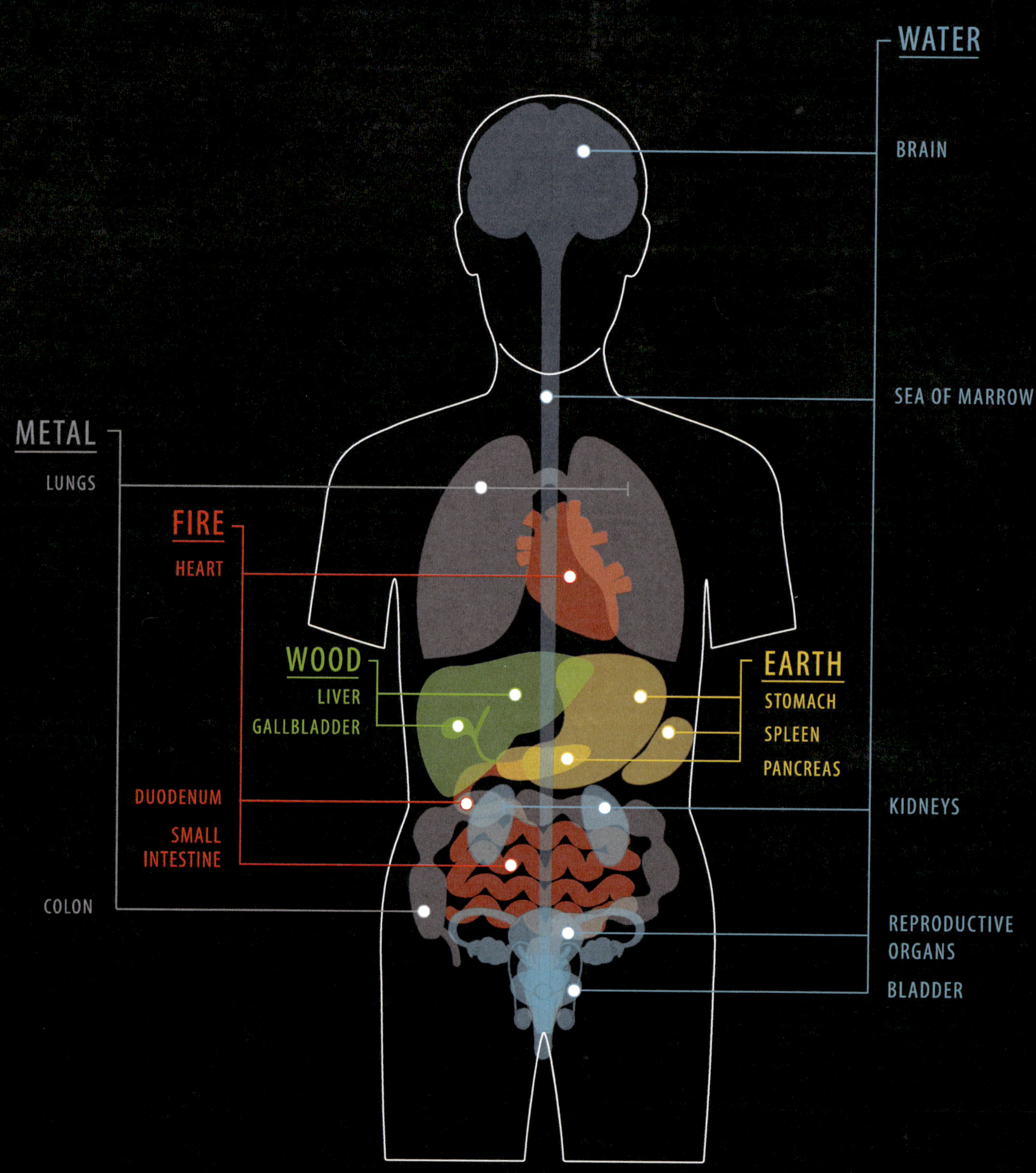

YOUR FIVE ELEMENTAL SPIRIT ORBS

The five yin–yang organ alliances and energetic orbs in your Sacred Tree are nurtured by the Spirits of Wood, Fire, Earth, Metal, and Water. They are the elemental Spirits' powerful processors, responsible for synchronizing the seasons, high-frequency vibrations, low-frequency vibrations, and a plethora of other cyclical wonders of living and thriving as a spirit in a human incarnation. Hence, the Spirits of Wood, Fire, Earth, Metal, and Water activate your evolutionary impulse at a specific juncture in Nature's cycle, working together in an eloquent and expressive sequence. In other words, each organ group and energetic orb in your Sacred Tree is a spoke in the wheel of life, which is ignited by the regenerative power of Nature's elemental Spirits, not unlike water in a water wheel.

YOUR ANCIENT ELEMENTAL AND CYCLICAL WISDOM

For centuries, Chinese shamans and medical Qigong and traditional Chinese medicine (TCM) practitioners have elaborated on the interconnectivity of the human experience with all other living beings and the regenerative cycle of Nature. Their observations and insights are a vibrant reminder that harmony and well-being are not a fixed ideal; they are ever-changing and evolving states you co-create with Nature and all living beings, including the earth and the sun. Their wisdom and flow charts help you remember the rhythm of Nature and your corresponding physical, emotional, mental, and spiritual tides. Harmony in summer, for instance, is very different than harmony in winter. At any given moment, harmony expresses itself as one flavour of equilibrium in the great enterprise of living well at a particular juncture in Nature's omnipresent regenerative cycle.

YOUR INNATE HEALERS: THE HIGH-FREQUENCY EMOTIONS

Emotional energetic currents have different vibrational rates, ranging from high-frequency emotional states to low-frequency emotional states. The high-frequency emotions are the living expression of your innate elemental Spirits: Wood, Fire, Earth, Metal, and Water. Thus, these spiritual guides, referred to as pre-natal virtues in medical Qigong and TCM, are imprinted in your five energetic orbs before birth. They not only raise the vibratory rate of your physical body and energetic orbs but also bolster the transformational and healing power of each energy orb in Nature's regenerative cycle. Thus, these healing agents boost your capacity to transcend dis-ease and trauma, including sexual abuse. In other words, when you tune in to and nurture their power, you unleash your intrinsic capacity to set harmony into motion.

YOUR LOW-FREQUENCY EMOTIONS

When you avoid, suppress, or deny low-frequency emotions, they accumulate within your body and energy bodies, thereby creating disharmony. Thus, the stockpile of low-frequency emotions in your organs weakens your energetic fields and vice versa. Consequently, your life force contracts and flows incorrectly. Please note that the maelstrom of painful emotions experienced in traumatic circumstances in and of themselves do not set disharmony into motion, but it's the buildup of neglected low-frequency emotions that creates disharmony and illness. It's important to make this distinction. When flowing, all emotions create harmony, including the low-frequency ones:

a. The fluid expression of anger can provoke the creation of healthy boundaries and motivate you to right some wrongs.

b. The fluid expression of excitement can foster happiness and relaxation.

c. The fluid expression of worry can instigate introspection, preparation, and change.

d. The fluid expression of sorrow can disperse grief, relieve distress, or instigate beneficent concern and action.

e. The fluid expression of fear can stimulate healthful vigilance and discerning self-protection.

HIGH- AND LOW-FREQUENCY EMOTIONS

ELEMENTS	WOOD 木	FIRE 火	EARTH 土	METAL 金	WATER 水
SEASONS	Spring	Summer	Late Summer	Autumn	Winter
YIN ORGANS	Liver	Heart	Spleen Pancreas	Lungs	Kidneys Brain Reproductive Organs
YANG ORGANS	Gallbladder	Duodenum Small Intestine	Stomach	Colon	Bladder Sea of Marrow
EXTERNAL ORGANS	Eyes Third Eye	Tongue	Mouth	Nose	Ears
HIGH-FREQUENCY EMOTIONS	Compassion Love Benevolence Kindness Patience Unselfish Actions	Inner Peace Order Contentment Pleasure Courtesy Forgiveness	Trust Honesty Faith Openness Imagination Stability	Integrity Honour Justice Dignity Generosity Social Responsibility	Wisdom Cognizance Willpower Quietude Restfulness Fluidity
EXPLOSIVE LOW-FREQUENCY EMOTIONS	Anger Rage Intolerance Hatred Resentment Stubbornness	Agitation Anxiety Excitement Restlessness Mania Arrogance	Abandonment Obsessiveness Workaholism Competition Covetousness Instability	Excessive Grief Guilt Greed Control Affluence Exploitation	Fear Terror Panic Horror Victimization Endangerment
IMPLOSIVE LOW-FREQUENCY EMOTIONS	Powerlessness Hopelessness Despair Depression Purposelessness Addiction	Heartache Longing Loneliness Codependence Self-Sacrifice Dissociation	Worry Regret Self-Doubt Remorse Suspicion Diversion	Shame Sorrow Disappointment Stinginess Self-Pity Pessimism	Disorientation Overwhelm Stagnation Aloneness Insecurity Paranoia

YOUR INNATE ELEMENTAL HEALERS IN ACTION

Each yin–yang organ group and energetic orb is imprinted with the elemental Spirits' physical, emotional, mental, and spiritual life-giving vibrations to process your suffering and transform it into wisdom. Reminiscent of your chakras and dantians, each yin–yang energetic orb in your Sacred Tree is a hospital, staffed with very dedicated, competent, and specialized doctors and personnel. As such, each energetic yin–yang orb in your Sacred Tree is a reliable source of high-frequency elemental medicine and guidance:

a. Your liver and gallbladder host love and compassion specialists.

b. Your heart and small intestine host inner peace and tranquility specialists.

c. Your spleen/pancreas and stomach host trust and honesty specialists.

d. Your lungs and colon host dignity and generosity specialists.

e. Your kidneys/brain/reproductive organs and bladder/sea of marrow host wisdom and clarity specialists.

Therefore, when adversity strikes, each energetic orb acts as a shock absorber for the energies in direct opposition to their optimal vibration and specialty. Despite your overwhelmingness and confusion, your elemental Spirits and energetic partners actually make sense of the chaos and host the low vibrations they are most equipped to re-integrate, transform, and heal. Thus, your Sacred Tree's energetic orbs reliably absorb your suffering in their healing facilities to comfort and heal your traumatized astronauts and architects of survival.

The traumatized astronauts are the aspects of your spirit, your soul fragments, who catapult out of your heart and Sacred Tree into a drifting trauma capsule when overwhelming adversity strikes. It stands to reason that when you are overcome by spiritual, mental, emotional, and/or physical pain, you lose sight of the pool of unconditional love in your heart and Sacred Tree. The traumatized astronauts' counterparts, the architects of survival, are the valiant knights in shining or not-so-shining armour created by the traumatized astronauts to survive the adversity using whatever resources they can pull together under duress. In other literature, they are often referred to as "coping" or "survival" mechanisms—but that description, in my opinion, belies how incredibly brilliant, beautiful, and lovable they really are.

Mercifully, your Sacred Tree's capacity to heal is constant, unless your Sacred Tree ecology is consciously or unconsciously neglected, overwhelmed, and faltering due to cumulative traumatic experiences or unwholesome activities. If this is the case, the five energetic orbs can become besieged hospitals with waiting rooms full of traumatized astronauts and architects of survival awaiting treatment from inundated personnel and doctors. Hence, it's the backlog crowding your hospital waiting rooms that cumulatively decreases the effectiveness of your innate elemental healers.

Thankfully, when a "hospital"—an orb or an organ group—hosts a logjam of untreated traumatized astronauts and architects of survival, it raises a white flag in the form of sensations and discomfort. If this message is not acknowledged, it produces more obvious imbalances and pain. And if again these stalwart emissaries are ignored, your Sacred Tree ecology will produce illnesses with as many bells and whistles as you need to heed their plea for your conscious and active engagement with neglected or suppressed low-frequency emotions.

This plot unfolds to ensure your growth and evolution. Unless you catch up with your abandoned traumatized astronauts and architects of survival as well as the love and life curriculum you are consciously or unconsciously overlooking, relief will only be temporary. In contrast, when you revitalize your overburdened teams with rest, nutritious food, meditation, self-inquiry, a physical practice unifying body–mind–spirit, and cleansing, your innate high-frequency emotions, teachers, and healers become accessible again. You then have the fuel you need to escort your traumatized astronauts and architects of survival back to health.

Let the Spirits of
Wood, Fire, Earth, Metal, and Water
do the heavy lifting for you!
Choose your reading, pull some cards,
and open up to the elemental
Spirits' blessings!

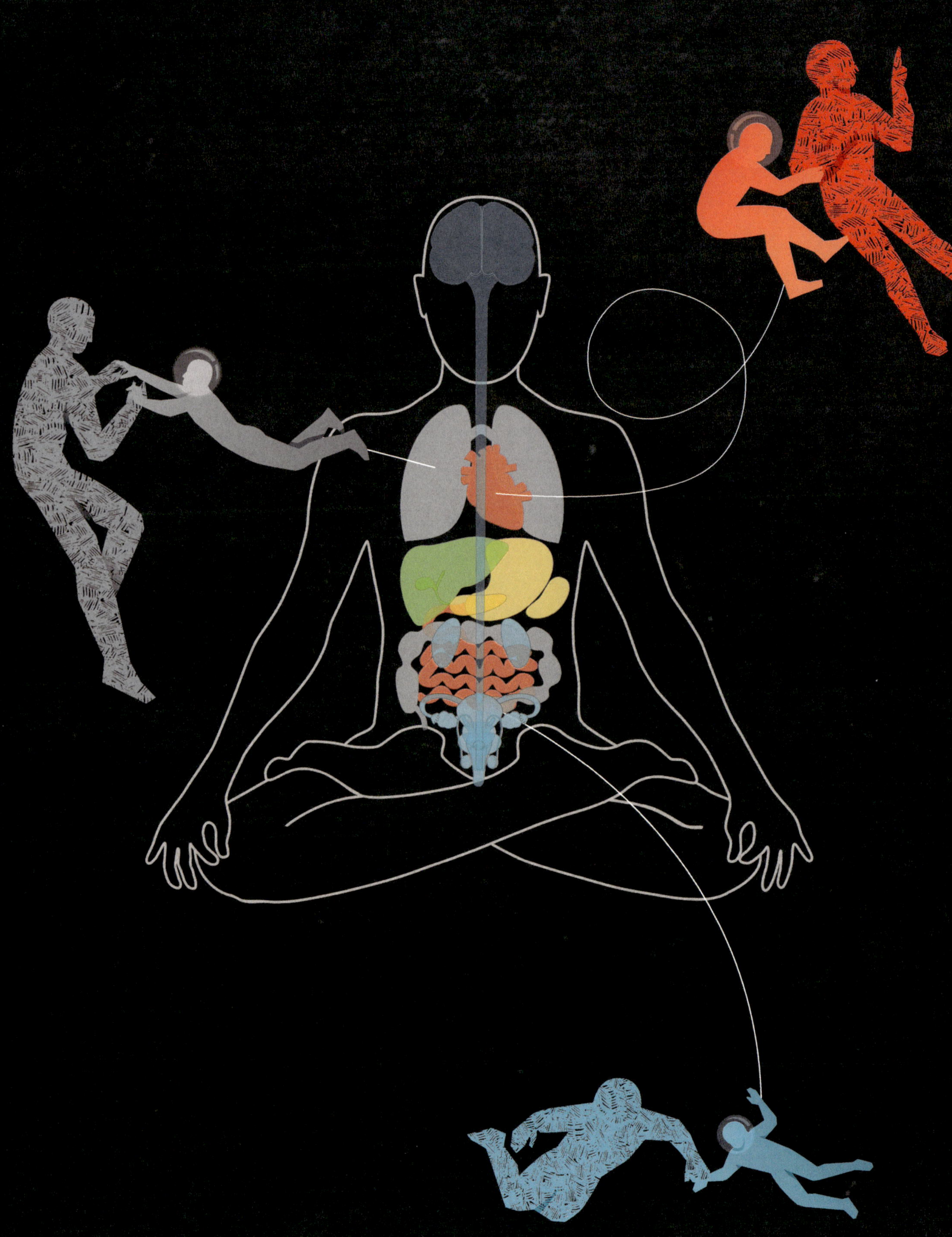

Elemental Spirits in Action

SACRED TREE HARMONY IN ACTION

WOOD	FIRE	EARTH	METAL	WATER
木	火	土	金	
1	13	25	37	49
Wood in spring shakes your Sacred Tree awake and inspires you to grow, change, and evolve. You are propelled forward with clarity, determination, and courage.	Fire in summer inspires you to love and be loved. Fire enchants you with the vigour and wisdom of her synchronized receiving and sharing cycle. You love, serve, move, sparkle, and play.	Earth in late summer spurs you to restore and self-heal your foundation. Your roots embody, more than anything else, your interdependence with all living beings, including the earth.	Metal in autumn buttresses your dignity and generosity. You recognize the might of a wholesome in-and-out flow and, conversely, the negative impact of attachment and accumulation.	Water in winter invites you to meet your unadorned essence and seedbed of all life. You rest, repair, and regenerate. You flow and adapt with ease.

Physical

HARMONY IN ACTION

WOOD	**FIRE**	**EARTH**	**METAL**	**WATER**
木	火			
2	**14**	**26**	**38**	**50**
You are mindful of what you put in your body and cleanse accumulated toxins. Your Sacred Tree grates against everything that constricts your evolution. Your intuition flows and you flow with its messages.	You sustain a wholesome self-care and self-love program. You take notice when your habits and outer life drown out your heart's sacred genius and service. You speak up and set healthy boundaries.	You are grateful for your physical body's wisdom and generosity. You have faith in its competence and self-healing prowess. You readily open to its counsel and act on its guidance. You eat well, rest well, and sleep well.	You accept change and aging. You do not participate in the corporate proliferation of products or therapies, exploiting your or others' fear of aging. Your fluid breath is a conscious exchange with all living beings.	Your earth body merges with Nature's robust rhythms and wisdom. You flow with the seasons. You listen and act on their guidance. Your activities and hormones calibrate accordingly.

DISHARMONY IN ACTION

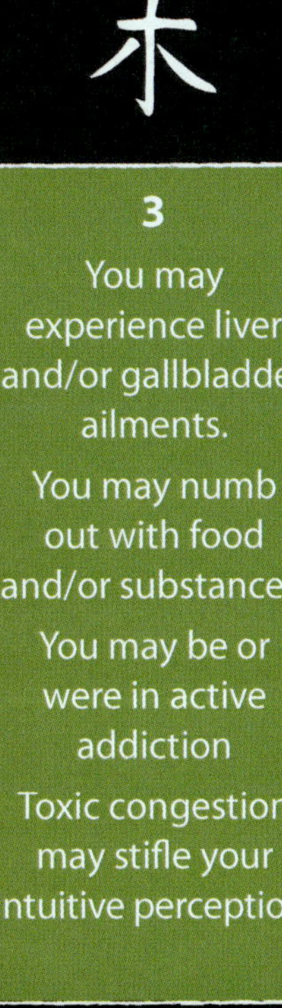

WOOD	FIRE	EARTH	METAL	WATER
木	火	土	金	水
3	**15**	**27**	**39**	**51**
You may experience liver and/or gallbladder ailments. You may numb out with food and/or substances. You may be or were in active addiction Toxic congestion may stifle your intuitive perception.	You may experience heart, duodenum, and/or small intestine ailments. You may keep going despite heart and abdominal disturbances. You may say yes when you mean no. You may be sinking in unlove.	You may experience spleen, pancreas, and/or stomach ailments. You may demand too much of your body or neglect it. You may be overactive or underactive; you may overeat or undereat; you may overperform or underperform.	You may experience lung or colon ailments. Your sense of self and your place in the world may be shaky or rigid. You may feel stuck or unyielding. You may swallow your feelings.	You may experience kidney, bladder, brain, reproductive organ, or sea of marrow ailments. Your hormones may be out of sync with Nature's cyclical wisdom. Flight–fight–freeze may capsize your wisdom.

Emotional

HARMONY IN ACTION

WOOD	FIRE	EARTH	METAL	WATER
木	火			
4	**16**	**28**	**40**	**52**
You invite a shift of tide and with it a release of stockpiled low-frequency emotions. Compassionate witnessing brings in a new level of awareness, patience, kindness, and benevolence.	You nurture your "Yes," the wellspring of your inner peace. You embrace your truth unconditionally and embrace others and their truth unconditionally too. You speak truth and convey truth.	You are robust and resilient and bend in the wind rather than snap or be uprooted. You trust yourself and trust the earth and the sun. You surround yourself with trustworthy people who support the development of your creativity and life path.	You greet grief and soften into its inevitability. You embrace beginnings and endings, death and rebirth. You appreciate the magnitude and payback potential of change and transformation.	Your stillness and serenity buoy you when you need to step it up and get out from under whatever thumb is oppressing you. You nurture your confidence, courage, and willpower. You live your dreams, NOT your fears.

EXPLOSIVE DISHARMONY IN ACTION

WOOD 	FIRE 	EARTH 	METAL 	WATER 
5 You, elders, and/or ancestors were/are oppressed, tormented, and/or colonized. Your intuitive perception may be bombarded or agitated by violence.	**17** You may be in shock due to an excessive load of challenging events. You may avoid acknowledging abuse. You may be criticized, harassed, controlled, colonized, and/or violated in the name of love.	**29** You may feel unworthy and alone in the world. You may feel abandoned, rejected, vilified, and/or censured. You may be destabilized by a human-centric personal, economic, and geopolitical narrative.	**41** You may have lost your moorings. You may be inconsolable, morose, exhausted, and/or apathetic. You may evade grief and potential disappointments. You may never cry.	**53** You may live in an environment saturated with discrimination and abuse. You may be criticized, harassed, controlled, and/or violated in the name of "natural," social, or divine order.

IMPLOSIVE DISHARMONY IN ACTION

WOOD 	FIRE 	EARTH 	METAL 	WATER 
6 You may be sinking in despair, depression, and toxicity. You may be tormented by your past or, conversely, you may avoid your pain. Your victim narrative may veil your intuitive perception and luminescence.	**18** You may get lost in others and become codependent. You may expect others to prop you up. Your truth may be silenced. You may propagate a constructed mythology, whitewash your past, and/or suppress your truth.	**30** You may be perilously busy. You may perform excessive chores and/or work overtime without adequate support or recognition. Others' expectations may drain you. You may suppress your emotions and numb yourself with activity.	**42** You may be tormented by shame and/or humiliation. You may feel inferior, tainted, scorned, and/or reprehensible. Shame may suffocate your dignity, self-worth, and/or accountability.	**54** You may be anxious and/or fearful most of the time. You may easily become flustered, overwhelmed, rattled, and/or intimidated. You may often back down from opportunities to grow. You may be brow-beaten verbally.

Mental

HARMONY IN ACTION

WOOD	FIRE	EARTH	METAL	WATER
木	火			
7	**19**	**31**	**43**	**55**
Your resolve to meditate and reflect is vivacious. You see yourself and others in a new light. You dynamically reinvent yourself or revitalize your genius and service.	You listen closely to the wisdom of all the elements, organs, elders, and teachers. You create order, make decisions, and wield power gracefully. You share your wisdom generously.	You dedicate an adequate amount of time and energy to your intellectual, creative, and activism ventures, as well as your outdoor adventures. You work and nurture yourself simultaneously. Sustainability is a built-in prerequisite.	You capitalize on your genius for the betterment of the world. You focus on mindful and ethical objectives, production, and distribution. Profits do not influence or distort your genius, objectives, and service.	You feed your faith and devotion in stillness and meditation to starve F.E.A.R. (False Evidence Appearing Real). You avoid fearmongering narratives and sensationalist media.

EXPLOSIVE DISHARMONY IN ACTION

WOOD	FIRE	EARTH	METAL	WATER
木	火			
8 Self-loathing and self-hatred may strangle your intuition and thwart your recognition of your genius and service. You may believe that you are inferior, bad, weird, pathetic, and/or incompetent.	**20** You may be restless, seek stimulation, and/or crave thrills or extravagance. You may belligerently rebel to gain freedom and power. Your voice may be loud, overly seductive, and/or controlling. You may bury your feelings with excessive stimulation.	**32** Your authentic inspiration and imagination may be hijacked by your quest to gain external validation, financial rewards, or prominence. You may push to get ahead rather than nurture your genius and service.	**44** You may define your self-worth with your job, house, lifestyle, or material gain. You may tend to be jealous and covetous. You may prioritize accumulation over relevance and service.	**56** You may believe that others will fall apart if you are not there. You may overwork to feel relevant, respected, or loved despite evidence to the contrary. You may latch on to validation and legitimization.

IMPLOSIVE DISHARMONY IN ACTION

WOOD	FIRE	EARTH	METAL	WATER

9 You may be confused and overwhelmed. You may be overmanaged, colonized, and/or under the sway of "isms." You may not see yourself as an independent and sacred being.	**21** You may be anxious, frenzied, or overactive. You may be saddled by others' needs, expectations, rules, and/or fiscal goals. You may seek others' validation and/or approval in lieu of love. You may say "Yes" when you mean "No." You may have panic attacks.	**33** You may inhabit manufactured realities and fantasies more vividly than your own. You may indiscriminately consume fantasies and information on social media, the Internet, TV, and in movies. You may hunger for the ideals portrayed.	**45** Scarcity and fiscal concerns may smother your aspirations, genius, and service. Your genius may be cut off from the "air" it needs to thrive and serve. You may remain in thankless or abusive jobs.	**57** You may believe that others are more intelligent, capable, or equipped than you are. You may believe that you are weak or broken. You may not hear yourself think past the din of doctrines, propaganda, and/or relentless chatter.

Spiritual

HARMONY IN ACTION

WOOD	FIRE	EARTH	METAL	WATER
木	火	土		
10	**22**	**34**	**46**	**58**
You incarnate love and compassion and live by the light of their teachings. You recognize your innate capacity to transcend the cycle of violence. You receive the earth's and the sun's stalwart messengers and guides.	Your laughter fosters the benevolent manifestation of your genius and service. You do what you love and love what you do. You nurture yourself and others. You honour who you are, fill your shoes, and honour others in theirs.	You trust the earth and the sun, and in turn you are trustworthy. You invite her teachings through your bare feet. You foster your enthusiasm, curiosity, creativity, imagination, and playfulness as well as those of others. You transcend geopolitical borders.	The earth's and the sun's abundance flows into the world via your committed and dynamic materialization of your genius and service. You transcend prevailing and imperious commerce with creativity, insight, and grace.	Your evolution mirrors the earth's and the sun's wise cycles. You flow with the potency of your genius and service. You listen to the earth's and the sun's stalwart messengers.

EXPLOSIVE DISHARMONY IN ACTION

WOOD	FIRE	EARTH	METAL	WATER
木	火			
11 Your lifework may be hijacked by agendas harmful to other living beings. You may be dominating, aggressive, and violent. Your intuition may be assaulted by real and/or fabricated violence.	**23** You may tend to chase highs. You may bypass emotions with meditation. You may crave spiritual fireworks, superiority, and/or veneration. You may preach or defend obstinately.	**35** Others or/and their cultures may interfere with the development of your spirituality, intellectual capacity, creativity, and/or imagination. You may be starved spiritually, intellectually, creatively, and imaginatively.	**47** Your desire to dominate and generate personal profit may be out of control. You may push to preserve or increase your gains, surplus, or hegemony even when they endanger other living beings.	**59** You may be mesmerized by the scarcity meta-narrative. You may be bewildered by the maelstrom of uncertainty and spiritual scarcity in the dominant culture. Your innate wisdom may be capsized by fearmongering.

IMPLOSIVE HARMONY IN ACTION

WOOD	FIRE	EARTH	METAL	WATER

12 You may be lost in a tangle of doctrines and social, cultural, and geopolitical rules and/or expectations. Your intuitive perception may be shrouded, or it's clear but you may be ignoring its messages.	**24** You may be self-sacrificing or selfless to a fault. Your faith's teachers or rituals may undermine your personal authority, power, and freedom. You may be hesitant to express your needs, beliefs, and truths. At worse, you may be trapped in a cult.	**36** You may be tragically cut off from the earth and the sun. Your screensaver may know the earth's natural wonders more than you do. You may be starved for time off in Nature. You may underestimate the power of rooting in the earth.	**48** You may be trapped in the vault of the economy, a human-made construct based on a capitalist and a colonialist framework. You may take what is precious and take it for yourself.	**60** You may be disoriented. You may persist in relationships and jobs despite dissatisfaction or abuse. You may be absorbed by narratives reinforcing the dominance and relevance of an external world order or security.

Imagery Lexicon

HARMONY IMAGERY

ELEMENTS	WOOD 木	FIRE 火	EARTH 土	METAL 金	WATER 水
SEASONS	Spring	Summer	Late Summer	Autumn	Winter
CELESTIAL BODIES	Rising Sun	High Sun	Setting Sun	Rising Moon	High Moon
HIGH-FREQUENCY EMOTIONS	Compassion Love Benevolence Kindness Patience Unselfish Actions	Inner Peace Order Contentment Pleasure Courtesy Forgiveness	Trust Honesty Faith Openness Imagination Stability	Integrity Honour Justice Dignity Generosity Social Responsibility	Wisdom Cognizance Willpower Quietude Restfulness Fluidity
HARMONY IMAGERY	Budding Sacred Trees progressing from bare branches to branches in full bloom and rising suns to express the initiatory vigour of the Spirit of Wood.	Flourishing Sacred Trees with chubby leaves, young fruit, and invigorating high suns to express the transformational might of the Spirit of Fire.	Bountiful Sacred Trees with powerful roots, ripening, scrumptious fruit, and setting suns to express the stabilizing and nurturing capacity of the Spirit of Earth.	Generous Sacred Trees with shedding leaves, rising moons, and abundant harvests ready for distribution to express the fortitude of the Spirit of Metal.	Quiescent Sacred Trees with still water and ladders connecting the earth and full moon to express the restorative yet expansive potency of the Spirit of Water.

DISHARMONY IMAGERY

ELEMENTS	WOOD 木	FIRE 火	EARTH 土	METAL 金	WATER 水
SEASONS	Spring	Summer	Late Summer	Autumn	Winter
CELESTIAL BODIES	Rising Sun	High Sun	Setting Sun	Rising Moon	High Moon
LOW-FREQUENCY EMOTIONS	Anger Intolerance Stubbornness Powerlessness Purposelessness Addiction	Anxiety/Shock Restlessness Arrogance Heartache Codependence Dissociation	Abandonment Obsessiveness Competition Worry Regret Self-Doubt	Excessive Grief Greed Control Shame Stinginess Pessismism	Fear/Panic Horror Victimization Overwhelm Stagnation Insecurity
DISHARMONY IMAGES	Piercing wooden spikes expressing the violence aimed inwardly or outwardly. Bound rising suns and white shrouds representing the choked initiatory power of your sacred relevance and intuition.	Shackled, exploding, or disintegrating stone towers expressing the contraction of your heart's truth whether you're spinning outward or inward. Either way, you're obscuring your heart's wisdom and song.	Gale-force winds, tornadoes, hurled fruit, and uprooted and felled trees to express the destructive impact of restricted, unfocused, agitated, competitive, or unethical production.	Desolate and truncated trees to express the misery and futility of attachment despite the inevitability of impermanence. Corporate towers and clear-cut forests to express the devastation of exploitation and stockpiling.	Perilous waterfalls, rushing water, and icebergs expressing the disruption of your seasonal repose and introspection. Broken ladders representing your disconnection from Nature's wisdom and cycles.

CHAPTER TWO

PULLING CARDS

HARMONY AND DISHARMONY CARDS: A CALL TO ACTION EITHER WAY

Chinese shamans and medical Qigong and TCM practitioners observe that all living beings are in a constant flux between harmony and disharmony or are sometimes navigating a virtual 50/50 blend. In light of this, harmony is never a *fait accompli*. At any given moment, you can experience harmony because you cultivate and support this balanced state, or conversely it can slip between your fingers because you neglect it. Thus, harmony is not interdependent with external circumstances deemed perfect, a privilege, a special aptitude, or a superior spiritual container. It is an active agent you grow or neglect. In other words, if you water your innate Sacred Tree, it grows; and if you neglect watering it, it withers.

Likewise, disharmony is never a given or fixed entity. For instance, it's not because you are slammed with adversity at a particular juncture that you are invariably plunged into disharmony. The state of disharmony is not interdependent with external circumstances deemed challenging, a built-in flaw, hard luck, or incompetence. Rather, it speaks of a fleeting or tenacious disorientation and confusion. Basically, you are in a state of disharmony when your requisite connection to the earth and the sun is ignored, disrupted, and/or obstructed.

Take heart, though. No matter what is happening or has happened to you, you remain a Sacred Tree and are connected to the rhythms of Nature. No amount of torment can disrupt your interconnectivity with Nature's primary orientation and progression. Although it feels like it sometimes, it's actually impossible to escape it. For example, when your spirit inhabits a physical body, this body will age and eventually die. Although this built-in underpinning can be unsettling, your Sacred Tree's impulse to grow and blossom is just as certain. In other words, all the subtle or grand manifestations of harmony are just as palpable and accessible as the seemingly unpreventable disharmony.

Mercifully, you are a magnificent Sacred Tree no matter how extreme your circumstances or suffering. While harmony is not something you can take for granted once you experience it or achieve it, the same can be said of disharmony. You can always count on your innate capacity to transform unlove into love, even when it seems delirious to think so.

EXPLOSIVE VERSUS IMPLOSIVE DISHARMONY CARDS

I chose to express the divergence from harmony in these oracle cards and the guidebook as either explosive or implosive—a flavour of disharmony is either more explosive than harmony or more implosive than harmony. Chinese shamans and medical Qigong and TCM practitioners traditionally gauge disharmony by measuring its variation from the ideal and harmonious midpoint. Hence, explosive versus implosive indicates in what direction the emotional, mental, or spiritual imbalance is going, from mildly explosive or implosive to excessively explosive or implosive. Please note that I do not itemize explosive or implosive physical disharmonies. A large body of information is available on hot and cold Imbalances in TCM texts and other resources.

HARMONY expresses your innate capacity to align with the earth and the sun.

Hence, pulling a Harmony Card suggests that you cultivate this specific flavour of harmony at this time.

You are in a state of DISHARMONY when you are not in sync with your innate Sacred Tree-ness.

Hence, pulling a Disharmony Card informs you of the likely source of your confusion and suffering while suggesting that you cultivate this specific flavour of harmony at this time.

HOW TO INITIATE A READING

1. RELAX.

Breathe, meditate, stretch, or do whatever is necessary to calm turbulence.

2. HOLD THE DECK IN YOUR HANDS.

Connect with the cards and offer gratitude to this tool and channel for the Spirits of Wood, Fire, Earth, Metal, and Water to work with you.

3. FORMULATE YOUR QUERY.

Consider what you would like to learn from this reading to formulate a juicy yet focused question. If nothing comes to mind, simply open your heart and offer up your curiosity and willingness to receive guidance from the Spirits of Wood, Fire, Earth, Metal, and Water.

4. SELECT A CARD SPREAD.

Look through the card spread diagrams to choose the reading you think will most generously reflect the insights and guidance you seek. Still, if you are short for time, choose the one-card Feedback spread. If you have twenty minutes to half an hour, then choose one of the two-card or three-card spreads: Alliance, Imprint, Challenge, or Metamorphosis. If you have an hour or more, then you have enough time to explore the Manifestation spread.

5. SHUFFLE THE CARDS.

You can shuffle the cards as you would a deck of playing cards or lay the cards face down on a surface and shift them around—whatever opens you up to receive the elemental Spirits' messages. Keep the cards' images hidden from you, sustain mindful presence, and keep focusing on your query. If a card jumps out at you during this process, set it aside. These teachings are clamouring for your attention and are especially relevant now.

6. PULL THE DESIGNATED NUMBER OF CARDS.

Pick the number of cards necessary for your reading and set them down in the numerical order of the spread you selected. Reveal the images in sequence by turning the cards right side up—this deck does not have reverse card readings.

7. OPEN TO GUIDANCE.

Soften into your guided self-inquiry. Observe the images on the cards and later refer to the charts and text describing the message each card offers. The Spirits of Wood, Fire, Earth, Metal, and Water are delighted to have an opportunity to share their compassion, dedication, and wisdom with you. The consciousness of each element is as enthusiastic as it is steadfast in its desire to see you grow and evolve into your full potential and magnificent Sacred Tree.

8. MEDITATE AND DO SELF-REIKI.

I highly recommend you take the time to meditate and do self-Reiki on the organs and elemental energy orbs that came up in your reading. If you do not have time, photograph your spread, tag the relevant pages, take notes, and return to it later.

Create the time and space for the Spirits of Wood, Fire, Earth, Metal, and Water to work with you. While the cards transmit their guidance and blessings, the Spirits' healing potency is in your hands, literally!

FEEDBACK SPREAD

CARD 1: STATE OF BEING AND THE SELF-HEALING RESOURCES YOU HAVE NOW

This card reveals your current state of being.

If you pull a ***Sacred Tree*** card, this Spirit's elemental teachings and pulse are super activated now and present healing opportunities on all levels: physical, emotional, mental, and spiritual.

If you pull a ***Harmony*** card, it reveals the teachings and rhythm you need to maintain and encourage at this time.

If you pull a ***Disharmony*** card, it reveals your most pressing imbalance. Look up the ***Harmony*** card in direct relationship with this imbalance. For instance, if you pulled the *Spirit of Wood Explosive Emotional Disharmony* card, look up the *Spirit of Wood Emotional Harmony* card description. Focus on the high-frequency emotions of this element to invigorate these innate healers at this time. You will receive insights as to how to apply it to your circumstances and query.

ALLIANCE SPREAD

CARD 1: STATE OF BEING

The first card reveals your current state of being.

If you pull a ***Sacred Tree*** card, the Spirit's elemental teachings and pulse are super activated now and present healing opportunities on all levels: physical, emotional, mental, and spiritual.

If you pull a ***Harmony*** card, it reveals the teachings and rhythm you need to maintain and encourage at this time.

If you pull a ***Disharmony*** card, it reveals your most pressing imbalance.

CARD 2: ALLY AND TEACHER

The second card reveals the greatest influence on your state of being.

If you pull a ***Sacred Tree*** or ***Harmony*** card, it reveals a stalwart ally. This harmony runs deep. You may recognize this guidance as a wholesome pattern in your life in general or in this particular era or circumstance. Maintain or encourage these high frequencies, receive their grace, and move forward trusting that their wisdom is with you.

If you pull a ***Disharmony*** card, it reveals that you have worked with this imbalance in the past. In that sense, this disharmony is now your teacher. You are encouraged to remember that healing journey and use the wisdom you integrated in the past to meet your current challenge.

PLEASE NOTE:

If the cards are in the same element, it indicates that this element's teachings are instrumental to your query. Read the detailed depiction of the ***Sacred Tree*** card if you are not familiar with this element's fundamental expression of harmony.

IMPRINT SPREAD

CARD 1: STATE OF BEING

The first card reveals your current state of being.

If you pull a ***Sacred Tree*** card, this Spirit's elemental teachings and pulse are super activated now and present healing opportunities on all levels: physical, emotional, mental, and spiritual.

If you pull a ***Harmony*** card, it reveals the teachings and rhythm you need to maintain and encourage at this time.

If you pull a ***Disharmony*** card, it reveals your most pressing imbalance.

CARD 2: IMPRINTED PATTERN

The second card reveals an entrenched harmonious or disharmonious imprint.

If you pull a ***Sacred Tree*** or ***Harmony*** card, it reveals that you have a solid and vibrant relationship with her high frequencies and rhythm. You may recognize her teachings as a wholesome pattern in your life in general or in this particular era or circumstance. Encourage this familiar wisdom now.

If you pull a ***Disharmony*** card, it reveals that this disharmonious pattern is persistent and is entangled with your current state of being. The good news is that you now have the resources to tackle this old foe. Look up the ***Harmony*** card in direct relationship with this imbalance. For instance, if you pulled the *Spirit of Water Implosive Mental Disharmony* card, look up the *Spirit of Water Mental Harmony* card description. Focus on the high-frequency emotions of this element to invigorate these innate healers at this time. You will receive insights as to how to apply it to your circumstances and query.

PLEASE NOTE:

If the cards are in the same element, it indicates that this element's teachings are instrumental to your query. Read the detailed depiction of the ***Sacred Tree*** card if you are not familiar with this element's fundamental expression of harmony.

CHALLENGE SPREAD

CARD 1: STATE OF BEING

The first card reveals your current state of being.

If you pull a ***Sacred Tree*** card, the Spirit's elemental teachings and pulse are super activated now and present healing opportunities on all levels: physical, emotional, mental, and spiritual.

If you pull a ***Harmony*** card, it reveals the teachings and rhythm you need to maintain and encourage this year.

If you pull a ***Disharmony*** card, it reveals your most pressing imbalance.

CARD 2: CHALLENGE

The second card speaks of the task, contest, or adversity you are facing.

If you pull a ***Sacred Tree*** or ***Harmony*** card, it reveals a vital need to focus on this wisdom and rhythm at this time. It's a challenge because you're back here *again*. You have met this teacher before but haven't consistently integrated the message or manifested the teachings yet.

If you pull a ***Disharmony*** *card*, it reminds you of a task you may find intimidating or formidable. That said, rest assured, it's in the forefront because you are ready to move forward on your evolution curriculum. It may also be a wake-up call or a plea to embolden your approach to a familiar hurdle or barrier. Regardless, it's time. Go for it!

CARD 3: GUIDANCE

The third card reveals your greatest influence on your imminent challenge and evolution.

If you pull a ***Sacred Tree*** *or* ***Harmony*** card, it suggests that you actively manifest her vital teachings now. You may recognize this element's teachings as a wholesome and activated pattern in your life in general or in this particular era or circumstance. Encourage this familiar wisdom now, receive its grace, and move forward trusting that these teachings are with you.

If you pull a ***Disharmony*** card, it reveals that you have worked with this imbalance in the past and released its pattern and imprint. In that sense, this disharmony is now your teacher. You are encouraged to remember that journey and use the wisdom you integrated to meet your current challenge.

PLEASE NOTE:

If the cards are in the same element, it indicates that this element's teachings are instrumental to your query. Read the detailed depiction of the ***Sacred Tree*** card if you are not familiar with this element's fundamental expression of harmony.

METAMORPHOSIS SPREAD

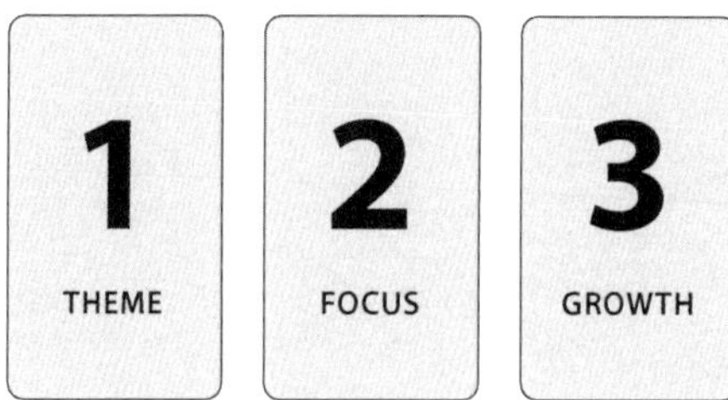

CARD 1: THEME

The first card offers insights into the major theme of your year ahead.

If you pull a ***Sacred Tree*** card, the Spirit's elemental teachings and pulse are super activated now and present healing opportunities on all levels: physical, emotional, mental, and spiritual.

If you pull a ***Harmony*** card, it reveals the teachings and rhythm you need to maintain or encourage this year.

You are offered this treasure trove of high frequencies to fuel, support, and inform your evolution on all levels: physical, emotional, mental, and spiritual. Don't let this gift atrophy. Embolden your endeavours and embrace growth and transformation. Get out of your own way! Resistance is futile.

If you pull a ***Disharmony*** *card*, it reveals your most pressing imbalance and challenge this year. Disharmony is not static. In other words, this is not bad news. This disharmony is a gateway to your metamorphosis. Trust the initiatory power of whatever adversity, contest, or challenge you are facing. You have an opportunity to discover, remember, and activate your capacity to transform these low-frequency emotions into high-frequency emotions.

CARD 2: FOCUS

The second card offers insight into what you need to do as a next step.

If you pull a ***Sacred Tree*** or ***Harmony*** card, it invites you to prioritize this fundamental body of high frequencies at this time. This key is on your keychain. Be alert and strategic. Use it. Apply the teachings to everything you do.

If you pull a ***Disharmony*** card, you are invited to surrender to an imminent initiation. A gateway is opening before you. Rest assured, this seemingly intimidating, painful, and/or scary enterprise is on the agenda because you have the resources to embrace this initiatory and transformational opportunity. How you approach it will in large part determine how intense or prolonged the process will be. Look up the ***Harmony*** card in direct relationship with this imbalance. For instance, if you pulled the *Spirit of Water Implosive Mental Disharmony* card, look up the *Spirit of Water Mental Harmony* card description. Focus on the high-frequency emotions of this element to invigorate these innate healers at this time. You will receive insights as to how to apply it to your circumstances and query. Let the ritual begin!

CARD 3: METAMORPHOSIS

The third card offers insights into who you are in the process of becoming.

If you pull a ***Sacred Tree*** *or* ***Harmony*** card, it reveals the potency of wisdom you can tap into if you embrace your program generously. You stand to gain a great deal by surrendering to the manifestation of the wholesome energies guiding you and letting go of the unwholesome imprints thwarting you.

If you pull a ***Disharmony*** *card*, it indicates that you will have gained the necessary knowledge and fortitude to meet another initiatory growth period. Although this may seem like a bummer, it isn't. You are receiving a meaningful vote of confidence. Furthermore, this growth spurt may take longer than a year, especially if you're living in menopause (or *man-opause*) or in one of your three Saturn returns (at ages twenty-eight, fifty-six, and eighty-four). All three Saturn returns are momentous portals when the planet Saturn completes a full orbit around the sun and returns to the same zodiac sign it was in when you were born. Saturn, the whistleblowing taskmaster of the skies, bolts in to highlight the disharmonies and blockages in your life. It insists you wise up, make judicious choices, and recognize your genius and service now. The more perilously distracted, stubborn, or unplugged you are, the more daunting the initiation tends to be. Although you may slither away and hide from it for a few years, there's no getting away from it entirely. You're important, even if you don't yet realize the far-reaching implications of your sacred relevance.

PLEASE NOTE:

If the cards are in the same element, it indicates that this element's teachings are instrumental to your query. Read the detailed depiction of the ***Sacred Tree*** card and refer to the charts if you are not familiar with this element's fundamental expression of harmony.

MANIFESTATION SPREAD

CARD 1: STATE OF BEING

The first card reveals your current state of being in relationship to your endeavour.

If you pull a ***Sacred Tree*** card, the Spirit's elemental teachings and pulse are super activated now and present healing opportunities on all levels: physical, emotional, mental, and spiritual.

If you pull a ***Harmony*** card, it reveals the teachings and rhythm you need to maintain or encourage at this time.

If you pull a ***Disharmony*** *card*, it reveals your most pressing imbalance.

CARD 2: CHALLENGE

The second card speaks of a task, contest, or process built in to your endeavour.

If you pull a ***Sacred Tree*** or ***Harmony*** card, it reveals a vital need to focus on this wisdom and rhythm at this time. It's a challenge because you're back here *again*. You have met this teacher before but haven't consistently integrated the message or manifested the teachings yet.

If you pull a ***Disharmony*** *card*, it reminds you of a task you may find intimidating or formidable. That said, rest assured, it's in the forefront because you are ready to move forward on your evolution curriculum. It may also be a wake-up call or a plea to embolden your approach to a familiar hurdle or barrier. Regardless, it's time. Go for it!

CARD 3: HIDDEN INFLUENCES

The third card speaks of hidden, unconscious, or negated influences relevant to your endeavour.

If you pull a ***Sacred Tree*** or ***Harmony*** card, it reveals that you have an important ally sitting in the wings. It suggests that you have an unacknowledged or neglected cache of resources and insights. Step into your wisdom. Recognize it and dance to its rhythm. It's important to embrace it and manifest it now.

If you pull a ***Disharmony*** card, it reveals a subterranean imbalance you are not aware of or addressing. It's crucial to recognize this disturbance, especially if it's systemic or chronic. Either way, it's time to push the rock aside to see what lies behind, even if it makes your skin crawl to think about it. You have the resources to do it now. The other cards in this spread will remind you of who your allies are and what resources you have now and present a viable path to freedom and well-being.

CARD 4: GUIDANCE

The fourth card reveals your greatest ally for this endeavour.

If you pull a ***Sacred Tree*** or ***Harmony*** card, it suggests that you not only integrate these teachings but also meet your challenge with active manifestation of these vital teachings. You may also recognize this element's teachings as a wholesome pattern in your life in general, or in this particular endeavour. Encourage this wisdom, receive its grace, and move forward trusting that its teachings are with you.

If you pull a ***Disharmony*** card, it reveals that you have worked with this imbalance in the past and released its pattern and imprint. In this sense, this disharmony is now your teacher. You are encouraged to remember that journey and use the wisdom you integrated to inform your approach and process.

CARD 5: ACTION

The fifth card reveals a need to focus these teachings and act now.

If you pull a ***Sacred Tree*** or ***Harmony*** card, it suggests that your efforts are buoyed by this element's might and potency now. Actively manifest this vital wisdom and rhythm now. Apply the teachings to everything you do. Your energy fields are aligned with this magnificence. Raise your sail and catch its generous wind.

If you pull a ***Disharmony*** card, it suggests that you work to redress this imbalance now. Whether it's old, chronic, scary, frustrating, intimidating, or feels hopeless, trust that this is the time to get on it. You are not alone. Energies are aligned to help you move through it and transcend this limitation.

PLEASE NOTE:

If the cards are in the same element, it indicates that this element's teachings are instrumental to your query. Read the detailed depiction of the ***Sacred Tree*** card if you are not familiar with this element's fundamental expression of harmony.

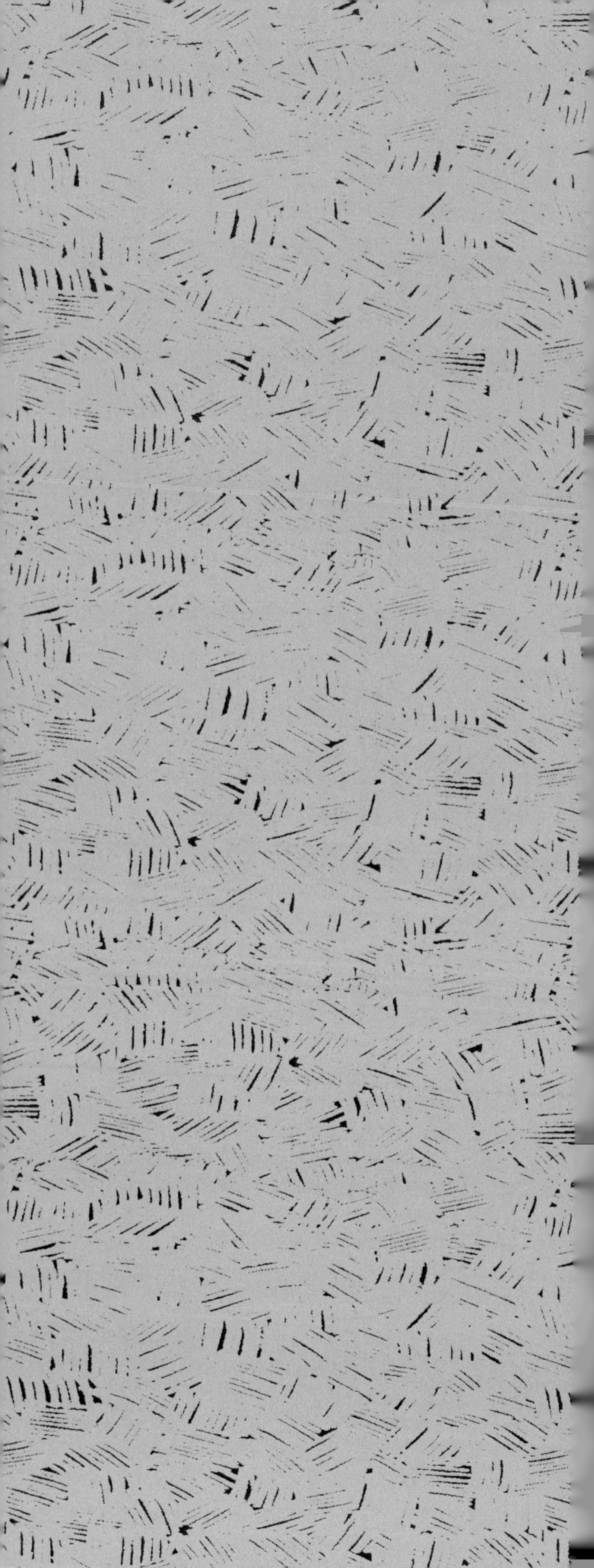

CHAPTER THREE

SPIRIT OF WOOD

SPIRIT OF WOOD

COLOUR	SEASON	YIN ORGAN	YANG ORGAN	EXTERNAL ORGANS
Green	Spring	Liver	Gallbladder	Biological Eyes Third Eye

WOOD ATTRIBUTES	SPRING PULSE
Cognizance of Your Genius and Sacred Relevance Comprehension of Your Past Recognition of New Possibilities Strategic Planning Change, Transformation, and Evolution	Capitalize on Nature's vivacious energy. Wake-up, shake down, and grow. Be bold despite growing pains. Face uncertainties and risks. Create, make things, do things, and begin again.

HARMONY	EXPLOSIVE DISHARMONY	IMPLOSIVE DISHARMONY
HIGH-VIBRATION EMOTIONS	EXPLOSIVE LOW-VIBRATION EMOTIONS	IMPLOSIVE LOW-VIBRATION EMOTIONS
Compassion Love Benevolence Kindness Patience Unselfish Actions	Anger Rage Intolerance Hatred Resentment Stubbornness	Powerlessness Hopelessness Despair Depression Purposelessness Addiction

WOOD	HARMONY	DISHARMONY
PHYSICAL	**2** You are mindful of what you put in your body and cleanse accumulated toxins. Your Sacred Tree grates against everything that constricts your evolution. Your intuition flows and you flow with its messages.	**3** You may experience liver and/or gallbladder ailments. You may numb out with food and/or substances. You may be or were in active addiction. Toxic congestion may stifle your intuitive perception.

WOOD	HARMONY	EXPLOSIVE DISHARMONY	IMPLOSIVE DISHARMONY
EMOTIONAL	**4** You invite a shift of tide and with it a release of stockpiled low-frequency emotions. Compassionate witnessing brings in a new level of awareness, patience, kindness, and benevolence.	**5** You, elders, and/or ancestors were/are oppressed, tormented, and/or colonized. Your intuitive perception may be bombarded or agitated by violence.	**6** You may be sinking in despair, depression, and toxicity. You may be tormented by your past or, conversely, you avoid its pain. Your victim narrative may veil your intuitive perception and luminescence.
MENTAL	**7** Your resolve to meditate and reflect is vivacious. You see yourself and others in a new light. You dynamically reinvent yourself or revitalize your genius and service.	**8** Self-loathing and self-hatred may strangle your intuition and thwart your recognition of your genius and service. You may believe that you are inferior, bad, weird, pathetic, and/or incompetent.	**9** You may be confused and overwhelmed. You may be overmanaged, colonized, and/or under the sway of "isms." You may not see yourself as an independent and sacred being.
SPIRITUAL	**10** You incarnate love and compassion and live by the light of their teachings. You recognize your innate capacity to transcend the cycle of violence. You receive the earth's and the sun's stalwart messengers and guides.	**11** Your lifework may be hijacked by agendas harmful to other living beings. You may be dominating, aggressive, and violent. Your intuition may be assaulted by real and/or fabricated violence.	**12** You may be lost in a tangle of doctrines and social, cultural, and geopolitical rules and/or expectations. Your intuitive perception may be shrouded, or it's clear but you ignore its messages.

LIVER – GALLBLADDER – EYES – THIRD EYE

SPIRIT OF WOOD

Sacred Tree in Spring

1

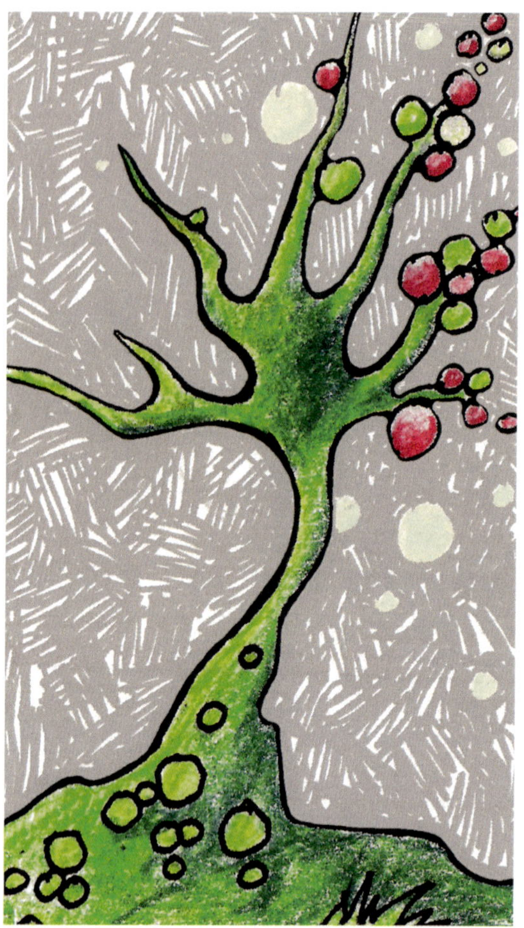

The Spirit of Wood shakes your Sacred Tree awake and inspires you to grow, change, and evolve!

1

As the days become warmer and brighter, the Spirit of Wood awakens. Your Sacred Tree, which has been at rest, storing and concentrating its energy under a winter blanket, voraciously draws water up from the earth through your roots and pushes this revitalizing essence into your trunk and branches. Like a snake ready to shed an old skin, the Spirit of Wood cajoles you into slithering upward and outward to split and scour off your constrictive year-old bark. This potent rebirth of energy scrapes against everything constricting your Sacred Tree.

Moreover, spring's brighter and longer days light your way to see yourself, other people, and situations with new eyes. Whether it's painful or scary to see aspects of your past differently or daunting to accept unpalatable truths about yourself, others, or situations, the Spirit of Wood encourages you to take advantage of these insights. She emboldens you and propels you forward with determination and courage despite potential growing pains or discomfort.

Furthermore, the Spirit of Wood helps you see new possibilities in your future. She invites you to dynamically reinvent yourself and embrace, revitalize, and/or expand the manifestation of your genius and sacred relevance. It is the perfect time to look ahead, make decisions, and determine your direction for the upcoming summer, year, or five years. No need to fret, though. Although every new growth and undertaking is accompanied by uncertainties and risks, the Spirit of Wood fortifies your sense of direction, strategic planning, and decision-making skills. She unfailingly stacks your odds. She makes sure you have what you need to move forward eagerly with grace and magic. And don't forget, it is your Sacred Tree's nature to surge forth, grow, and begin anew. Go for it!

The Spirit of Wood inspires you to step into your sacred relevance, make things, do things, and begin again.

LIVER – GALLBLADDER – EYES – THIRD EYE

SPIRIT OF WOOD
Physical Harmony
2

The Spirit of Wood inspires you to nurture your Sacred Tree's physical vehicle!

The Spirit of Wood shakes your Sacred Tree awake and stokes your capacious and audacious ability to grow, manifest your genius, and evolve. It's spring, after all; the earth is moist, the sun shines bright, and the Spirit of Wood grates against everything blocking your evolution. Moreover, she calls on you to support your transformation by mindfully ingesting wholesome nutrients and making a concerted effort to physically cleanse periodically, especially in the spring. Your most powerful filters, your liver and gallbladder, count on you to embrace the opportunity to scour off accumulated toxins and burdensome limitations.

Consequently, your third eye and intuitive perception flow more easefully too. You see your innate genius and life path and stay on track despite pressure and/or seemingly compelling social, cultural, and dogmatic beliefs contradicting love and compassion. Thankfully, you also intuit the steps necessary to align with your sacred relevance whether circumstances are pleasant, challenging, or oppressive. And most importantly, you invite, welcome, and witness all emotions and intuitive insights as they arise, including stagnant or suppressed low-vibration emotions and traumas.

Respect your Sacred Tree in all of its magnificence by nurturing it and filtering out foods, substances, and activities obstructing your sacred relevance.

LIVER – GALLBLADDER – EYES – THIRD EYE

SPIRIT OF WOOD

Physical Disharmony

3

You may be overwhelmed by toxicity and violence!

The Spirit of Wood beseeches you to recognize the power you have to mindfully seek foods and stimulation that embolden rather than weaken your Sacred Tree. She encourages you to take stock of what foods, substances, and stimulation you ingest consciously or unconsciously, voluntarily or involuntarily.

- Do you ingest foods or substances that burden your liver and gallbladder?
- Do you numb out with food and/or substances?
- Are you in active addiction?
- Are you bombarded with fabricated or real violence, victimization, and injustice in your home, community, or in the media?

3

The Spirit of Wood is here to reassure you that despite adverse conditions, you can strengthen your Sacred Tree ecology by being selective of what you consume. Whatever is being done to you, the Spirit of Wood entreats you to explore what you are doing to yourself. She motivates you to choose wholesome foods, substances, activities, and media, especially when you are under duress.

Violence—whether real, fabricated, or sensationalized in films, video games, or media—tends to cloud your intuitive perception and restrict your capacity to act on its wisdom. For instance, even if there is a way out, when your third eye is besieged by unwholesome foods or substances and/or violence, you may not see your way out or act on it. Your intuition may be so static-y or faint that either you do not receive intuitive messages or you receive them but do not act on them. Unfortunately, repetitive exposure to violence may also cause you to focus on your hardships and victimization and incite you to define yourself accordingly. Either way, your sacred relevance gets stuck in the mud.

Choosing wholesome nutrients for your body and mind is a bold first step toward greater personal power, authority, and clarity.

DISHARMONY STORY

You were a dynamic, productive, and passionate student, artist, and activist. You kicked ass for a couple decades, but who's counting. You were strong as a bull. Your body was solid, resilient, and virtually unstoppable. And if your body dragged, your will would climb right over it and keep on going, no matter what. This included colds, flus, infections, injuries, and hangovers (yeah, lots of those!). But now you're really counting! The whole darn ride has come to a crashing halt. You can barely drag yourself out of bed. You can't digest a thing—food just goes right through you. You feel exhausted, shaky, and weak. You're haunted by your childhood victimization and overwhelmed by the brutality of it all. You're sinking in helplessness, powerlessness, and hopelessness. If truth be told, you've lost all hope of ever being out there alive and kicking again. "It's over, all of it!"

From breathing in and living off the heat of the explosive outrage that fuelled the client's renegade art and activist actions, their pendulum has crashed into the other end of the Spirit of Wood disharmony spectrum: implosive depression and dejection. Although they have done some healing, there's no shortage of trauma and lots more needs to be witnessed compassionately. Likewise, they are saddled with no shortage of physical mayhem: their pancreas isn't producing adequate enzymes and their healthy gut flora is so weak that they can't break down their food into nutrients they can absorb. These imbalances wreak havoc through their whole digestive track because food isn't in the form the various segments are designed to deal with. Besides being malnourished now, they grew up on junk food and later had no time or desire to cook or eat well. OUCH!

Moreover, it's clear that the client is numb. They are taking a number of antidepressants, antianxiety pills, sleeping pills, and a healthy dose of ethyl alcohol to wash it all down daily. None of it is new. Drugs and alcohol were always on the scene, but the problem is accumulated toxicity, escalation, and the pills altering their brain chemistry. They are cut off not only from their pain and accumulated low-frequency emotions but also from their genius and sacred relevance. They are sitting in a sailboat with the sail down. No amount of wind can get them going again if they don't raise their sail. Double OUCH!

The good news is that they can do something right now to feel somewhat better within a few weeks. Healing their liver, pancreas, and thirty feet of digestive plumbing will take some time and so will the trauma-processing enterprise. In addition, their Spirit of Wood bears the brunt of all the toxic foods, ethyl alcohol, and pharmaceutical and recreational drugs they ingested over their lifetime, plus occupational and environmental toxins such as insecticides, pesticides, and solvents. Nevertheless, they can unburden their Spirit of Wood, liver, gallbladder, pancreas, and brain chemistry by consuming less sugar (it's lethal) and other encumbering foods and substances. It doesn't matter where they start; the point is to start taking out some toxic stuff rather than adding in more toxic stuff.

One sure way to raise your sail and get your hands on the rudder is to unburden your Spirit of Wood. For instance, when your great filtering matriarch, your liver, is clogged, your blood is also encumbered. Cleaning your blood will support all organs, including your brain, and third eye. Mindfully ingesting and cleansing is often the first very powerful collaborative gesture with your body and Sacred Tree. It is an affirmative and intentional step in your life-changing act of self-transformation, actualization, and rebirth.

A clean-up operation or intervention starts with one action.
Each discerning action, no matter how small, gets you closer to your intuitive wisdom, genius, and sacred relevance.

LIVER – GALLBLADDER – EYES – THIRD EYE

SPIRIT OF WOOD

Emotional Harmony

4

The Spirit of Wood buoys you into an expansive rebirth!

The bright and dynamic manifestation of the Spirit of Wood in the spring revitalizes your innate high vibrations: love, compassion, generosity, kindness, and patience. The awakening of these robust allies and teachers can spur a powerful release of stockpiled low-frequency emotions.

- A budding or heightened hope releases you from the pull of low-vibration emotions.
- Pulsing new insights press against the strictures and limitations of your rigidity or resistance.
- Nascent green shoots push through your despair or bitterness.
- A warm spring breeze subdues your impatience or exasperation.
- Undulating life softens your aversions or hatred.
- Growing self-respect dilutes the bog of self-loathing and self-hatred.

Furthermore, the vitality and perspicacity of the Spirit of Wood inspires you to tackle the ongoing exigencies of facing truths inside and outside your day-to-day life. She encourages you to witness emotions and intuitive insights in the moment. She incites you to acknowledge accumulated low-frequency emotions and release yourself from their contraction and imprint regularly. And if the Spirit of Wood prompts you to remember repressed memories of traumatic events, you do so in her embrace, knowing you are strong enough to compassionately witness and integrate now.

The Spirit of Wood animates your innate capacity to cleanse, heal, and transcend emotional suffering.

LIVER – GALLBLADDER – EYES – THIRD EYE

SPIRIT OF WOOD

Explosive Emotional Disharmony

5

You may be sitting on a keg of dynamite!

Yowza! The Spirit of Wood beseeches you to take stock of the conditions pressurizing your Sacred Tree ecology. She inspires you to acknowledge that you may be oppressed, colonized, and/or abused or that you oppress, colonize, and/or abuse others. She encourages you to explore your elders' and ancestors' history too—they may have been oppressed, colonized, and/or abused or they oppressed, colonized, and/or abused others. Whether you are abused or an abuser, the Spirit of Wood is here with you now. She bolsters your strength and courage to compassionately witness your truth and your ancestors' truths and motivates you to brazenly, yet patiently, dismantle the cycle of violence one loving step at a time.

Furthermore, the Spirit of Wood prompts you to assess if your third eye is agitated by violence and if your perception of the world is governed by a comprehensive catalogue of danger, violence, victimization, and injustice.

- Do you witness systemic violence or exceptional attacks in your family, village, city, or nation?
- Do you study and/or work to shift the conditions of disenfranchised groups?
- Are you forced to witness violence?
- Do you seek sensational journalism produced for high ratings, entertainment, and shock value? Do you hook into the media coverage of progressing violent situations such as extreme cases of natural disasters, abuse, abductions, hostage-takings, serial murders, serial sex offences, and/or missing persons or unprincipled Holocaust pornography?

Regardless of the conditions, the Spirit of Wood beseeches you to make as many judicious choices as possible, especially if you are under duress. Clean up your smartphones, computers, desks, and night tables. Seek compassionate truth rather than sensationalized diversions, distractions, dogma, and/or propaganda. Most importantly, compassionately recognize the impact of the cycle of violence and create the conditions necessary for both victims and perpetrators (who are also victims) to heal.

The Spirit of Wood incites you to bring love and kindness wherever it is lacking.

DISHARMONY STORY

You grew up in one of the poorest neighbourhoods in the city. Your father was a tough disciplinarian who ruled the household with an iron fist. You were often abused physically, and you habitually witnessed your father abusing your sisters and mother. You walked on eggshells at the best of times and cowered in horror when subjugated to the patriarch's volatile will and violence. Moreover, you were abused sexually by a Catholic priest when you joined the choir. Come what may, you somehow discovered the vivacity of art and sought training in portraiture, regardless of familial resistance and financial constraints. Despite humiliation and suppression, a dream nudged you out of the mire.

Unfortunately, their newfound ecology of enthusiasm and passion was too fragile to withstand the dawn of abstract painting and the rebellious rejection of classical portraiture in particular. When all the plaster busts and statues as well as all the representational work by the school's students were vandalized, smashed, or thrown out the window, they never returned to train at this esteemed institution or sought other training. Add to this the timely tenacity of the person they wished to marry. To be deserving of their hand, they insisted they must make money rather than play with oil paint. They need not say more; off they went on what would turn out to be an impressive climb out of poverty to the higher echelons of the nouveau riche class in the late 1960s and 1970s. The economy was booming, and they rode the crest of the surge with unrelenting panache.

Within a decade, everything *nouveau* boosted their power and everything *riche* spiced up their swag. If it wasn't the perpetually soaring sales, it was the growing number of workers under their command; if it wasn't the new bungalow, it was the new pool (read: parties); if it wasn't the wine, it was the drugs; if it wasn't the Moulin Rouge feather and tit shows, it was the mistresses; if it wasn't their prize-winning ballroom moves, it was their newfound position as the head cock of the roost. Literally. Their fervour to sexually abuse their daughter unfortunately escalated: what started off as sporadic violent and drunken attacks escalated within three years into sexual servitude for yet another three years.

This man is not a client. He is my father and I am the girl who was enslaved. In spite of that, I'm perpetually in awe of his suffering. I mean, really think about it, the pain he inflicted is on him, not me! Sure, I suffered and believe you me, I was no angel. I flung a lot back. I created negative karma by the bushels as well. While the length and breadth of my transformative journey as a victim and perpetrator brings me to my knees, the healing journey ahead of him after death staggers even the most vivid imaginations. He has created thousands of dumpsters of harsh intensity to deal with. As hard as it is to face it ALL while alive, we actually have the opportunity to create wholesome karma out of bad. All of us. He unfortunately died without clueing in to this vital and transformative ecology.

My memoir, *ME TOO LOUD & CLEAR: How I Walked the Talk from Silence to Active Hope,* is as much about my father's tragic abuse as a child and the inevitability of further activating the cycle of violence when self-inquiry and self-healing are not embraced. I, more than anyone, witnessed the grisly play-by-play of my father's heartbreaking debacle. He was swallowed whole by the relentless fires of unresolved pain running amok in his body and cells. Violence, internal and external, is the inexorable outcome of turning a blind eye on his truth: not only traumas but his Sacred Tree. Conversely, if he had softened into compassionate self-inquiry and self-witnessing, he would have animated his Sacred Tree's capacity to transform unlove into love—unwholesome karma into wholesome karma.

In meditation, I often see in my mind's eye a Hindu swami, his shoulders hunched with both his hands up to his face, shaking his head as he compassionately witnesses the torrent my father has unleashed. I've been there in this lifetime and others, and most of you have been there—it's horrific. Yet, it's impermanent and just as alchemically charged with love as the path of healing from victimization. My father is loved. He is held. And he, too, is on the path to love, perpetrator or not. And at some point, he will receive the wholesome karma of this lifetime because there was some of that too, and with it, he'll stoke his Sacred Tree and clamber out of the cycle of violence. We're all in it together anyway—simultaneously playing out the epic human enterprise of healing back to love one way or another. No matter what side of the equation you are on, victim or perpetrator, you suffer. You not only hurt another human being but also create more suffering than you can imagine or predict by unwittingly creating more unwholesome karma and suffering in your future. In other words, you fuel the cycle of disharmony with potent and long-lasting reverberations.

Despite the intensity of your pain, the trauma or unwholesome karma is not an attack or punishment. It is love's fundamental impulse to give you another opportunity to gain wisdom and transcend the cycle of violence.

LIVER – GALLBLADDER – EYES – THIRD EYE

SPIRIT OF WOOD

Implosive Emotional Disharmony

6

You may be sinking into a morass of despair, depression, and toxicity!

Make haste, grasp for the Spirit of Wood now, for she is within reach! She gladly lends you her strength, courage, and clarity to buoy your spirit in this disheartening time. The Spirit of Wood compassionately witnesses that you may be consciously or unconsciously overcome by a menacing brew. There's nothing quite like a victim narrative mixed in with toxicity, stagnant low-frequency emotions, denial, and addictions to stifle your appreciation of your innate genius and sacred relevance. Whatever the proportions or conditions, the Spirit of Wood beseeches you to take stock.

- Do you feel worn down by the magnitude of adversity in your present or past?
- Do you focus almost exclusively on the hardships you have experienced and define yourself accordingly?
- Do you feel permanently damaged?
- Do you feel innately powerless or trapped in a victimizing world?
- Do you feel doomed to meet a tragic ending?

The Spirit of Wood acknowledges that you may be overwhelmed by a maelstrom of low-frequency emotions precipitated and sustained by unhealed trauma. You may be in denial, you may tend to minimize your traumatic history and emotions, or you may be addicted to numbing your traumatic history and emotions with substances, distractions, excitement, drama, causes, and/or co-dependent relationships. Whatever the circumstances or survival mechanisms, the Spirit of Wood encourages to reach out for her, for she will guide you on a journey back to your Sacred Tree, the aspect of you innately aligned with the high vibrations of love, compassion, kindness, patience, and benevolence.

The Spirit of Wood assures you that your Sacred Tree is not only your birthright, it is a towering giant, more sturdy and resilient than the cycle of violence itself.

DISHARMONY STORY

You have many drinks daily and have eaten virtually nothing but sugar and carbs for the past thirty years. You also take a lot of Tylenol and over-the-counter muscle relaxants with codeine: "I have to! With the constant headaches and sinusitis I've had for the past five years, it's hard to get anything done." In fact, you can't think most of the time because your tinnitus is also driving you crazy. You keep going to doctors and you get prescriptions for your sinuses, and antidepressants for your mood, and some antianxiety pills because you're a nervous wreck. And, oh yeah, some sleeping pills too because you can't sleep either.

Ay, caramba! How can they possibly feel well considering the scope of this chemical cocktail alone? Let's see now. Their headaches are actually many headaches at once. First, they drink enough ethyl alcohol and do so often enough to have hangovers daily, but they don't talk about that. Second, they take enough pills on top of the drink to create a massive backlog in their liver, but they or their doctors don't talk about that. Third, the booze, sugar, and carbs program has spawned a raging candida problem that expresses itself as bloating, sinusitis, and brain fog, but they or their doctors don't connect those dots either. Fourth, they have several old and unhealed concussions and neck injuries because their father hit them on the face and head repeatedly, but they really don't talk about that. In addition, their father abused them sexually, but they never talk about that because he told them they were dirty and liked it.

They are bamboozled and disoriented by their unhealed trauma, the collateral damage of physical, emotional, and sexual abuse, and a bewildering toxic brew. They are trapped in a vicious cycle: toxicity in their liver has adverse effects upon their emotional state, and their emotional turmoil and unhealed trauma impair their liver function and well-being. The liver and gallbladder are the innkeepers for the high vibrations of love and compassion as well as for most of the heavyweights at the other end of the spectrum, such as rage, hatred, resentment, apathy, hopelessness, self-loathing, humiliation, powerlessness, and horror. It's a total catch-22. These intense emotions are so painful and scary that it seems in their best interest to numb themself with pills and booze to hide the whole wicked lot under the guise of depression, but it invariably makes matters worse because the Spirit of Wood's beautiful high vibrations of love and compassion are also submerged.

Their depression is an implosive and repressive impulse on a rampage—when they are depressed, they are numb and therefore suppress a whole host of nasties, which seems like a good idea for a while. However, in the long run, they thwart their opportunity to process, integrate, and eventually transform their suffering into wisdom. In other words, they stay stuck in their crazy amount of pain and remain locked out of their Sacred Tree. I get it! For instance, if I hadn't been stoned out of my mind for the last four years I lived in my parents' house, I'm not sure where I'd be. If I'd remained just as stoned for the next few decades, though, I'm not sure where I'd be either. Addiction to substances, like every other architect of survival, serves your highest and greatest good for some time but not an indefinite amount of time. I'm aware that the word *addiction* implies that you are trapped in a vicious web of physical dependency, to name but one of the levels of dependency, yet this is precisely the point: every architect of survival worth its weight in gold is addictive specifically because you depend on them to survive!

Even when it comes to thinking about taking extreme measures and perhaps ending your life, this impulse is actually an architect of survival in high gear rather than an annihilating weakness or depression. Every ancestor I have met who took their own life did it in an attempt to survive—they killed themselves in a desperate attempt to survive the pain. In other words, it's the pain they really wanted to kill, not themselves. Although physical death successfully ended that specific expression of pain, they did not end their built-in impulse to learn and evolve. Hence, they are not as scot-free as anticipated. The karmic energy and love's curriculum come back in other forms in another life, and it can be even more challenging to transcend now that there is more unwholesome karma at play. My recommendation is to refrain from adding more unwholesome karma to the mix. Self-harm is just as violent and costly as hurting or killing someone else. Despite the extent of your suffering, you are as important and sacred as everyone else.

The Spirit of Wood celebrates your capacity to set yourself free and evolve in this lifetime! She emboldens your innate Sacred Tree with the gusto you need to transcend victimization and your impulse to numb or self-annihilate.

LIVER – GALLBLADDER – EYES – THIRD EYE

SPIRIT OF WOOD

Mental Harmony

7

The Spirit of Wood prompts you to actively cultivate mental vitality and clarity!

7

The Spirit of Wood invites you to acknowledge the perpetual tidal fluctuations of your mental state and incites you to navigate the swells consciously. Her vivacity fuels your resolve to practise meditation, self-inquiry, yoga or the equivalent, and/or outdoor activities to calm your mind. Her generous energy motivates you to cultivate patience, kindness, benevolence, love, and compassion more consistently. Mercifully, the more you practise, the more these high vibrations influence your choices and actions and the less your past trauma and victimization shape your self-perception and worldview.

Poignantly, the Spirit of Wood's get-up-and-go energy encourages you to slow down and regroup daily, monthly, and annually to retain your focus on mindful activity and your sacred relevance. She encourages you to use her energy wisely and teaches you to capitalize on her exuberance to manifest your genius. Appropriately, the Spirit of Wood blesses you with fluid and vibrant intuitive perception, thereby shining her light on your sacred relevance. As such, she increases your ability to steer with clarity and courage and helps you recognize the telltale signs of distraction and/or interference.

The Spirit of Wood fuels your capacity to embrace the enduring cycle of crisis, disorientation, meditative pause, self-inquiry, regained clarity, and reorientation.

LIVER – GALLBLADDER – EYES – THIRD EYE

SPIRIT OF WOOD

Explosive Mental Disharmony

8

You may feel pathetic and/or consumed by hateful thoughts!

Dang! Slow down, rest, or meditate! You're spinning in a muddled maelstrom of low frequencies powerful enough to obscure your life-sustaining vertical axis and relationship to the earth and the sun. The Spirit of Wood witnesses your bewilderment and lends you its roots, trunk, and branches to reorient your Sacred Tree.

- You may be under the influence of people who present a version of reality that does not match your subjective experience and/or justifies their disrespect, oppression, and/or violence toward you.
- Your sense of self may be so distorted that you believe that others are justified in treating you with disrespect and/or violence.
- You may be so browbeaten that you believe that you are justified in treating yourself with disrespect and/or violence.
- You may hate yourself but love your oppressor, or you hate your oppressor and hate yourself.

Unfortunately, self-loathing and self-criticism are formidable and stealthy foes. Their sneaky yet loud invasion of your mind crushes your capacity to recognize and respect your innate Sacred Tree-ness. These crazy-making adversaries garble your intuitive perception and with it your capacity to perceive and honour your magnificence and sacred relevance.

- You may believe that you are bad, disgusting, and/or weird.
- You may believe that you are inferior, stupid, and/or incompetent.
- You may believe that you are pathetic, weak, and/or sick.
- You may believe that you are incapable of taking action based on your own life force, initiative, and wisdom.

When you turn to the Spirit of Wood, she infuses your Sacred Tree with discerning insights to inspire and fuel your ascent beyond your disparaging beliefs.

DISHARMONY STORY

You hate your father. He physically, emotionally, and sexually abused you, and you watched him hit and humiliate your mother and both sisters. On a good day, you think of him as the preposterous jerk who ruined your life; and on days when you're in pain, he's the motherfucker who fucking got away with it. Either way, it's really intense. Besides, it's by hating "the fucker" that you overcame your helplessness when he attacked you: "I am powerless to stop whatever you are doing to me, but I can hate you and I will hate you until the day I die." Your hatred and resentment splatters on the walls of your misery and hopefully his too. It appeases you to see that it really hurts him to know that you all hate him. And come hell or high water, you're not going to let up—that's all the "asshole" deserves.

Is it all you deserve, though? Unfortunately, hating your abuser(s) backs you into a nasty corner. From where I sit as a survivor of sexual abuse, hatred is clearly not a sin or failure, it is your last-ditch effort at creating a boundary with your oppressor(s). Regrettably, until you transcend this valiant architect of survival and their brilliant strategy to create a boundary, this low-frequency emotion lives in you, not them: you! In other words, it hurts you more than it hurts them. For as long as you harbour hatred, you are trapped and remain in the clutches of the abuse and abuser, and your Spirit of Wood suffers.

Besides, you don't need to worry about holding your abusers accountable in this way. Karma is what I refer to as Divine Justice in my memoir, *ME TOO LOUD & CLEAR: How I Walked the Talk from Silence to Active Hope*. When I was digging myself out of the hole, I eventually sensed a colossal justice-minded knowing that permeated everything. I sensed that my grandfather's, father's, and mother's actions were acknowledged and wisely accounted for. I sensed that the truth was known; and I knew in my bones that if I released my hateful grip, I could get on with living, growing, thriving, and loving.

I can assure you that letting go of my hatred for my mother, father, and maternal grandfather not only set me on the heart-healing journey of radical forgiveness, but it actually paved the way for self-compassion and eventually for self-love. Hating them unintentionally fed the flames of self-loathing and submerged the Spirit of Wood's high frequencies for decades. It catastrophically thwarted my growth and sacred relevance—internal violence is no less violent than external violence.

8

The Spirit of Wood is with you every step of the way!

She compassionately witnesses your rage and disorientation, and she acknowledges the magnificence of your Sacred Tree and bolsters your capacity to grow, transform, and evolve back to love.

LIVER – GALLBLADDER – EYES – THIRD EYE

SPIRIT OF WOOD

Implosive Mental Disharmony

9

You may be in a state of confusion and overwhelm!

Whew, let the Spirit of Wood pick you up and remind you of the boundless power of your Sacred Tree! You may not recognize your innate capacity to grow tall and bright at this time. The Spirit of Wood compassionately witnesses that you may be trapped in a morass of chaos, uncertainty, and unlove so overwhelming that you may be face down in the mud.

9

- You may be under the sway of all sorts of "isms" telling you that you don't deserve equality or respect—that your rights, feelings, needs, desires, sacred relevance, and aspirations do not count.
- You may be overmanaged and/or colonized.
- You may prioritize other people's needs and sculpt your personality, interests, relationships, career, and behaviour to reflect their values, priorities, expectations, demands, and/or rules.
- You may live in someone else's fortress rather than in your innate fertile genius and sacred relevance.
- You may internalize the gaze of an oppressive, critical, or controlling person and see yourself through their eyes.
- You may learn to think like others in order to better predict and manage their reactions and act accordingly.

The Spirit of Wood acknowledges that under these conditions you may be unable to create a daily to-do list for the practical execution of basic maintenance and self-care and feel even less capable of strategizing and initiating the changes you need to make in order to cleanse, align, and manifest your sacred relevance. The Spirit of Wood generously lends you her strength and clarity to overcome the conditions crushing your growth potential and lucidity.

Rest assured, the Spirit of Wood loves you! She generously fortifies you and wholeheartedly substantiates your birthright to be a relevant, unique, independent, and sacred being.

DISHARMONY STORY

You get horrible headaches and migraines. You only go out if you have to, and some weeks you can barely keep up with your responsibilities at home. You have a whole slew of food sensitivities, often experience digestive upsets, and catch a lot of colds and flus. You don't fare well emotionally either. You swing back and forth between dejection and rage. One thing is for sure, you feel like a caged animal. You're married to a poised, caring, competent, and self-assured professional. Yet at home your partner is impatient, rude, and volatile. They never care what's happening to you unless one of your commitments, needs, expenses, desires, moods, or illnesses intrudes on their expectations, rules, or urges.

It's like that with everything, including sex. The client used to be at their partner's beck and call. Now they put them off for as long as possible. Yet how much longer can they delay the unavoidable? Because, truth be told, at some point it always becomes unavoidable: "I'm their partner, for God's sake; I have to do it at some point." "It's been more than three weeks; they've got to get it one of these days!" "We're on holiday, they have to get it at least once." "They've been sulking for a week; I have to suck it up." "It's not the time to rock the boat; there's lots going on this week already." "They're tired tonight, it's bound to be quick." "I've pushed it to limit; I have to give in tonight." "They're incensed; I have to do it now." "Okay, you win, let's do it." Despite their lack of desire, aversion, or, on some days, repulsion, they do it. They do what they have to do to mollify their partner and, most importantly, thwart their need to have an affair. "That's what happened to my mother, so there's no way it's going to happen to me. There's a price to pay!"

Yet the client does not tally the biggest price of all: the implosive loss of personal power, authority, and autonomy. They are trying to get their life on track. "The kids have left home, and I really want to get on with it. It's my turn!" This is precisely the point. For it to really be their turn, they need to be empowered consistently. The cost of dissociating and having out-of-body sex time after time is tremendous. To make matters worse, the client was abused sexually as a child. They are using the survival skills they learned in that context of victimization, and its mindset continues to sink its talons into their body–mind–spirit.

Even though they concede to their partner less and less, each time that they do, they also submit to the culture of rape. The impact of living in sexual servitude is underestimated, and so is the fact that we live in a culture that supports it openly, or secretly, or tacitly. They strengthen the internalized patriarchal beliefs that intercept their evolution and dream of self-governance.

They intensify the impact of the oppressive cultural biases inhibiting their personal power. They continue to decimate their self-worth. And they remain muddled about their personal and unique trajectory and purpose. They basically play into the hands of misogyny.

Yet they have it in them to say "No." The sad truth is that their partner is not going to do it for them and neither is the culture. Not yet, anyway. They have to take it upon themselves to own their whole being. And they will by stepping into their personal power and authority one healthy boundary at a time with fewer and fewer ifs, ands, or buts. The power of the Spirit of Wood is in their innate Sacred Tree!

The clearer you are, the more you activate your Sacred Tree and with it unleash your capacity to grow and release your sacred relevance into the world.

The Spirit of Wood assures you that stepping into your power and authority happens in one moment, then another, and another, and another.

LIVER – GALLBLADDER – EYES – THIRD EYE

SPIRIT OF WOOD

Spiritual Harmony

10

The Spirit of Wood entices you to wholeheartedly embrace your Sacred Tree's medicine!

The Spirit of Wood is the backbone of your fortitude, resilience, and alignment with your genius and sacred relevance. When inspired by her, your actions are creative acts of will in the service of healing, transformation, and the evolution of all living beings.

- You acknowledge the power you have to transform suffering into wisdom and love.
- You are empowered and make conscious choices each day to produce wholesome karma.
- You embody patience, kindness, benevolence, love, and compassion despite unpleasant, challenging, and/or violent setbacks or losses.

When you live by the magic and power of your Spirit of Wood, you honour your intuitive perception by nurturing and maintaining a clear channel. You avoid disruptive stimulation and you listen attentively and act on your hunches, sudden insights, dreams, and visions. You cultivate your innate ability to communicate with ancestors, angelic guides, spirit animals, and/or ascended masters. Hence, you thrive in collaboration with your guides.

- You see the big picture and the deeper meaning inherent in all things.
- You perceive and dismantle potential cages, obstructions, and limitations as they arise.
- You find solutions to problems more readily or spontaneously.

The Spirit of Wood inspires you to vivaciously align with your sacred relevance and stokes your innate capacity to transcend the cycle of violence despite adverse conditions.

LIVER – GALLBLADDER – EYES – THIRD EYE

SPIRIT OF WOOD

Explosive Spiritual Disharmony

11

Your sacred relevance may be hijacked by agendas harmful to other living beings!

The Spirit of Wood is here with you now in all of her magnificent power to reconnect you with your innate Sacred Tree in alignment with love, compassion, kindness, generosity, and benevolence. She embraces you magnanimously, whether you are a victim or a perpetrator or both. She compassionately witnesses your luminescence despite your suffering, the suffering you may cause others, and your confusion. Regardless of your actions, she respects you and honours your birthright to know love and manifest your sacred relevance.

- You may often be impatient, irritated, and/or frustrated.
- You may often be controlling, aggressive, and/or violent.
- You may often be intolerant, heterosexist, sexist, classist, ageist, and/or racist.
- You may be an indoctrinated employee, soldier, guard, or enforcer.

The Spirit of Wood also recognizes that your third eye may be assaulted by real and/or fabricated violence often enough to amplify your bewilderment. Unfortunately, witnessed violence, real or fabricated, is just as traumatic and destabilizing as experienced violence or perpetrated violence. The Spirit of Wood recognizes that the following conditions may heighten your turmoil and/or desensitize you to violence:

- You may helplessly witness frightening and violent scenes frequently or did so at a young age.
- You may witness others who are routinely humiliated, intimidated, harassed, controlled, persecuted, or enslaved or did so at a young age.
- You may be bombarded with potentially traumatizing, fabricated, designed, and/or real violence in sensationalized media, entertainment, and/or video games or were at a young age.

The Spirit of Wood is the backbone of your fortitude, resilience, and capacity to change, grow, and evolve. Her presence awakens your innate power to transform suffering into wisdom.

DISHARMONY STORY

You work in a high-stakes corporate environment. It's a dog-eat-dog world out there, but you think on your feet and learn the ropes swiftly. It's impressive. The folks at the top are making big bucks, and you're already making twice as much as you were a couple years ago. It's intoxicating. People look good, they get together after work, eat great food, drink fine wine, gain prominence in restaurants and nightclubs, go to high-profile concerts, sports events, and theatre, and hook up. It's fun. You're living the life you never thought possible, and you're really good at what you do.

But then rumours start flying. Although you are affronted and upset, you keep your head high and plow forth, figuring that the lies will eventually run out of steam. But they don't. In fact, they become so persistent and vicious that your personal and professional reputation is smeared. The doors that flew open are slamming in your face faster than you can keep up. At first, the bullying, slandering, and harassment is debilitating, but eventually outrage kicks in and its intensity fuels rebellion. You seek legal counsel, and sure enough, you have grounds for a class-action suit. You want justice and you are going do to whatever it takes to get it.

And they do. The client perseveres for more than a decade. On the one hand, they're researching, proving, documenting, countering, and emailing. On the other hand, they are raging, ranting, and raving. Consequently, they strain, flail, agonize, anguish, and despair. Unfortunately, it's not just boxes and boxes of legal documents and research they accumulate, it's low-frequency emotions by the truckload. Their Spirit of Wood becomes so burdened that the high-frequency emotions such as love, compassion, kindness, patience, and tolerance become inaccessible. Even though the client is fighting for rightful recognition and justice, they can nonetheless exacerbate their condition by also fixating on gaining power over the person who hurt them and/or hurting the person who hurt them. It's a very easy slip-up and overlap, especially when the plot has no shortage of twists and turns. Unfortunately, when you resort to "power-over," no matter the circumstances, your resourceful architect of survival is at risk of becoming a perpetrator. You can unwittingly climb down into the gaping jaw of the cycle of violence.

Medical Qigong practitioners say that although the heart stores the spirit, it is the liver that can unbalance the spirit. "No kidding—your spirit might as well be strapped to an electric chair!" A Spirit of Wood spiritual explosive disharmony rips through your capacity for kindness, generosity, and compassion. It thwarts your sacred relevance, hopes, and aspirations. It also feeds the illusion of separateness enough to conceal the life-sustaining fabric of your interconnectivity and interdependence with all other living beings, including animals, plants, rocks, and the planet.

11

Considering the agonizing intensity
it can stir up, it's no surprise
that a Spirit of Wood in explosive
disharmony can foster nothing less
than conflict, abuse, violence,
war, and even genocide.

When in doubt, turn to her for
guidance and inspiration to stoke
your innate capacity to be
compassionate, patient, and kind.

LIVER – GALLBLADDER – EYES – THIRD EYE

SPIRIT OF WOOD

Implosive Spiritual Disharmony

12

You may lose track of who you are, where you're at, and where it's at!

Yikes, you may have temporarily lost your way! The Spirit of Wood is here to fortify your fundamental vertical axis and interdependence with your dynamic and fundamental allies: the earth and the sun. Believe it or not, the formidable energy of rebirth is with you now. The Spirit of Wood encourages to be bold despite off-putting anticipation of growing pains, uncertainties, risks, or confusion. She assures you that your Sacred Tree, rooted in the core of your being, stands tall despite your subjugation.

- You may consistently look outward for guidance, knowledge, or wisdom.
- You may be lost in a tangle of doctrines, social, cultural, and geopolitical rules, conditions, and/or expectations.
- You may take it for granted that you must obey or submit to an external authority figure or ideology.
- You may be intimidated, harassed, controlled, persecuted, or enslaved.

Furthermore, your intuitive perception may be shrouded by conscious or unconscious social, cultural, and geopolitical biases. Your inner wisdom may be routinely discounted by oppressors and their dogma, lies, and manipulation. Therefore, your capacity to see clearly enough to align with your Sacred Tree's innate personal power and authority may be obscured.

- Abuse, violence, racism, or sexism in your home or workplace may be disguised or systemically repudiated.
- You may be told over and over again that what you see is not real.
- Your willingness to see truth may be hindered by your investment in the economy of the relationships, circumstances, or job.
- You may turn a blind eye to your own suffering, the suffering of others, or your own violent actions.

Even if this call to action gives you the willies, know that the Spirit of Wood is with you and injects you with the vitality and clarity you need to shake off whatever external force is regulating you. Lean on her. She's here to give you traction in project liberation and evolution.

DISHARMONY STORY

Your father has a volatile temper. Sometimes he spins out in a rage and blames everyone in sight for his misery. At other times, a yelling rampage is not enough; he reaches for any object in sight and rams into you or your mother or both of you at once. But your mother gets the worst of it. Their fights are more extreme and last longer, sometimes through the night. Then one day, you find your mother motionless on the kitchen floor. You had witnessed enough of your father's eruptions and violence, and experienced enough of it first-hand, to believe that you were seeing the incarnation of your greatest fear. Hence, the image of your "dead" mother "killed" by your father imprints on your retina. Within minutes, you lose most of your sight in one eye: "Now, I've seen it all and I've seen enough!"

In the blink of an eye, a powerful architect of survival swept in and made a huge and final decision to block 90 percent of this person's sight to protect them from seeing anything horrific ever again. Unfortunately, it wasn't only their left eye that shut down but their third eye too. Henceforth, they lived without really seeing. So much so that they did not acknowledge their volatile father sexually abusing their daughter between the ages of two and nine, despite catching him red-handed many times. They did not kick him out of the house or prevent him from having access to their child. They failed to witness the magnitude of the situation or their child's distress. Then again, when their husband—the child's father—sexually abused their daughter from the age of nine to fifteen, they saw without seeing. Eventually, when they realized that their daughter was pregnant, they even took the child to a physician, who accepted a large sum of money to perform an illegal and life-threatening abortion!

This story is not about a client. It's about my own mother, and I am the child whose pain she could not see. I'm aware of my mother's suffering in the spirit world. Still, five years after her death, she yearns to embrace me, knowing all too well that her failure to protect me also violated me. The brutality of her grief defies description. I am visited often by the exquisite white seabird that her soul has chosen as a vehicle in my dreams, visions, and meditations. She loved the sea. And she loved me, this is clear. However, clutching to the survival program she created on that hopeless day at seventeen belittled her capacity to compassionately witness not only her own pain but eventually her own daughter's pain. Her "blindness" crushed her innate ability to self-heal her wounds, protect her child, and transcend the cycle of violence. Tragically, she remained powerless and helpless until she died.

Intuitive perception is your built-in compass. Without it, your spirit can become so disoriented that you, too, end up doing the very thing that you thought unimaginable or, worse, unjustifiable.

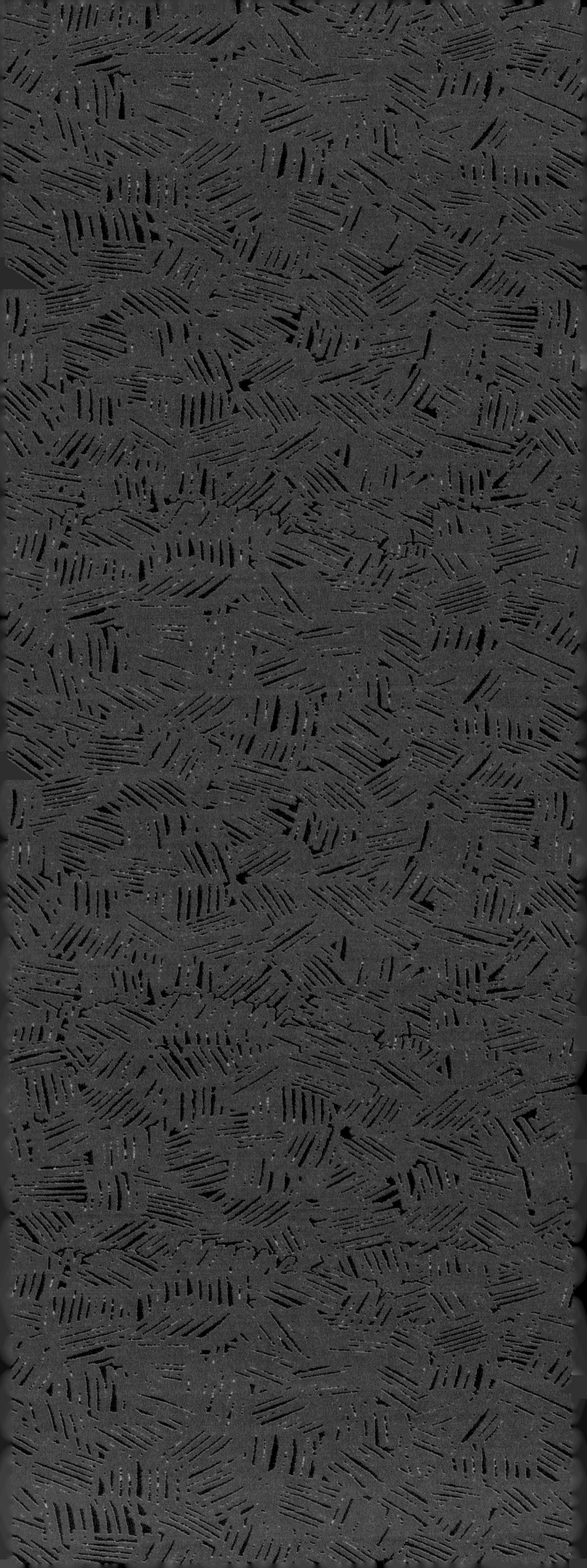

CHAPTER FOUR

SPIRIT OF FIRE

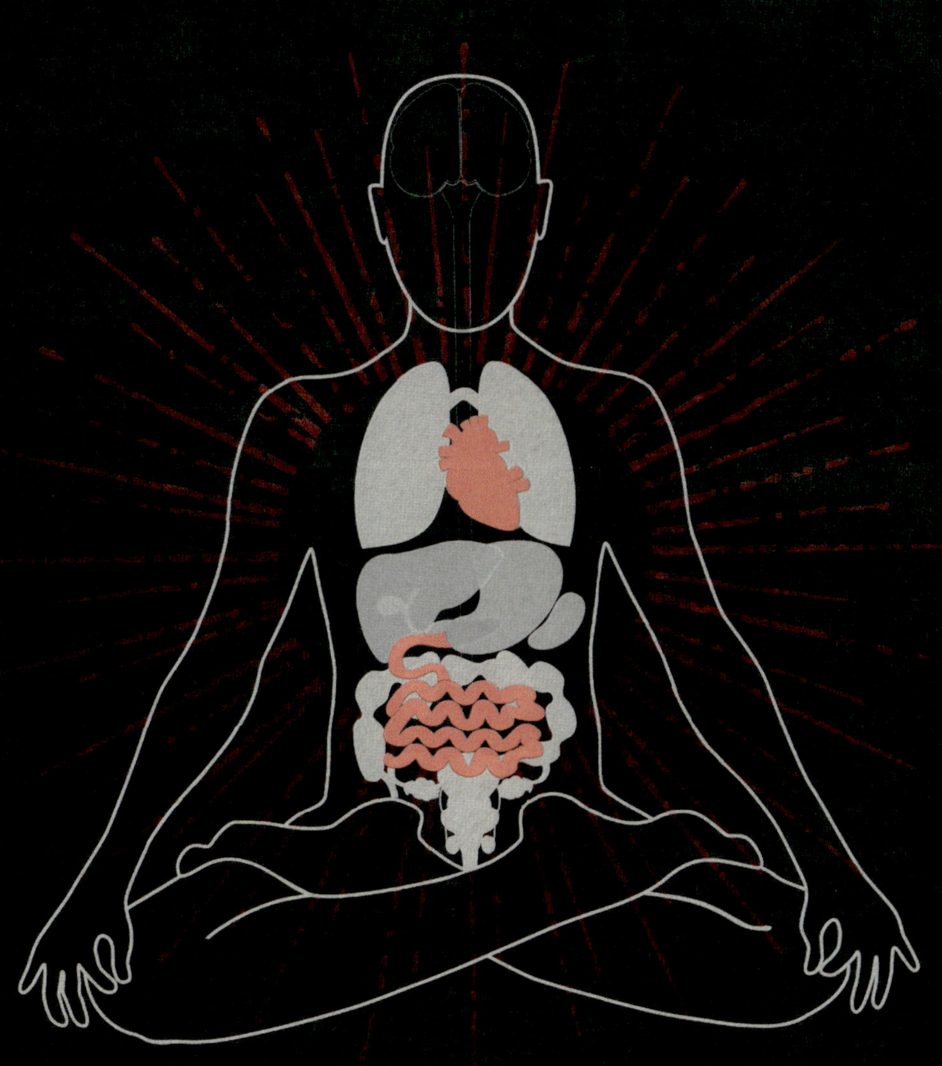

SPIRIT OF FIRE

COLOUR	SEASON	YIN ORGAN	YANG ORGANS	EXTERNAL ORGAN
Red	Summer	Heart	Duodenum Small Intestine	Tongue

FIRE ATTRIBUTES	SUMMER PULSE
Love and Self-Love Inner Peace and Abundance Sustainable Service Fulfillment and Contentment Enthusiasm and Laughter	Drink in the sun. Blossom and transmute your flowers into fruit. Manifest your genius into service. Be vibrant inside and out: speak up, sparkle, move, dance, run, and play.

HARMONY	EXPLOSIVE DISHARMONY	IMPLOSIVE DISHARMONY
HIGH-VIBRATION EMOTIONS	EXPLOSIVE LOW-VIBRATION EMOTIONS	IMPLOSIVE LOW-VIBRATION EMOTIONS
Inner Peace Order Tranquility Contentment Pleasure Forgiveness	Agitation Anxiety Excitement Restlessness Mania Arrogance	Heartache Longing Loneliness Codependence Self-Sacrifice Dissociation

FIRE	HARMONY	DISHARMONY
PHYSICAL	14 You sustain a wholesome self-care and self-love program. You take notice when your habits and outer life drown out your heart's sacred genius and service. You speak up and set healthy boundaries.	15 You may experience heart, duodenum, and/or small intestine ailments. You may keep going despite heart and abdominal disturbances. You may say yes when you mean no. You may be sinking in unlove.

FIRE	HARMONY	EXPLOSIVE DISHARMONY	IMPLOSIVE DISHARMONY
EMOTIONAL	16 You nurture your "Yes," the wellspring of your inner peace. You embrace your truth unconditionally and embrace others and their truth unconditionally too. You speak truth and convey truth.	17 You may be in shock due to an excessive load of challenging events. You may avoid acknowledging abuse. You may be criticized, harassed, controlled, colonized, and/or violated in the name of love.	18 You may get lost in others and become codependent. You may expect others to prop you up. Your truth may be silenced. You may propagate a constructed mythology, whitewash your past, and/or suppress your truth.
MENTAL	19 You listen closely to the wisdom of all the elements, organs, elders, and teachers. You create order, make decisions, and wield power gracefully. You share your wisdom generously.	20 You may be restless, seek stimulation, and/or crave thrills or extravagance. You may belligerently rebel to gain freedom and power. Your voice may be overly seductive and/or controlling. You may bury your feelings with excessive stimulation.	21 You may be anxious, frenzied, or overactive. You may be saddled by others' needs, expectations, and/or rules. You may seek others' validation in lieu of love. You may say "Yes" when you mean "No." You may have panic attacks.
SPIRITUAL	22 Your laughter fosters the benevolent manifestation of your genius and service. You do what you love and love what you do. You nurture yourself and others. You honour who you are, fill your shoes, and honour others in theirs.	23 You may tend to chase highs. You may bypass emotions with meditation. You may crave spiritual fireworks, superiority, and/or veneration. You may preach or defend obstinately.	24 You may be self-sacrificing or selfless to a fault. Your faith's teachers or rituals may undermine your personal authority, power, and freedom. You may be hesitant to express your needs, beliefs, and truths. At worse, you may be trapped in a cult.

HEART – DUODENUM – SMALL INTESTINE

SPIRIT OF FIRE

Sacred Tree in Summer

13

The Spirit of Fire entices you to love and be loved!

13

The Spirit of Fire in summer urges you to sweep down to Mother's warm earth to guzzle up her nutrients and inspires you to reach for the sun with your branches to imbibe her potency. Her heat licks awake every cell of your Sacred Tree. Her song reverberates through you, thereby infusing you with the cadence and magic of your sacred relevance. It's summer, after all; her Spirit graces you with the energy you need to transmute your flowers into fruit—your genius into service.

Thus ignited, the Spirit of Fire is the capacious energy of love and peace in action. She expresses herself in laughter and enthusiasm and charms you into living your service joyfully. And if you don't know what your service is, no worries: she encourages you to stay amused and keep looking. Either way, the cajoling Spirit of Fire persuades you to celebrate the fruition of your seeds large and small.

The Spirit of Fire also enchants you with the vigour and wisdom of her synchronized receiving-and-sharing cycle. She entices you to receive her blessings and then ignites you to share your blessings with others: to love and be loved. While she emboldens you to dip into your heart and gut to find what you can give to others unconditionally, she assures you that it's only when your inner fire burns bright and your inner peace runs deep that you can truly share your medicine in the world sustainably. As such, she continuously provokes you to nurture your inner fire, the aspect of her living in you. When you dance with the Spirit of Fire, your inner abundance flows outward easefully and sustainably while your fulfillment and contentment fuel your inner fire.

The Spirit of Fire inspires you to love, serve, sparkle, move, dance, and play. Be vibrant inside and out!

HEART – DUODENUM – SMALL INTESTINE

SPIRIT OF FIRE

Physical Harmony

14

The Spirit of Fire encourages you to embrace a self-care curriculum!

The Spirit of Fire inspires you to eat well, exercise regularly, and sustain wholesome routines so you can transmute your flowers into fruit. She motivates you to focus your attention on your heart's song and take notice when your food plan and activities drown out its sacred pulse. The Spirit of Fire urges you to pause and reflect—especially when the health of your biological heart, duodenum, or small intestine falters—and to pay attention when you feel nervous and anxious or you experience a lack of fulfillment, contentment, or pleasure.

She encourages you to identify:

- the foods disrupting your digestion;
- the habits and activities that tend to overexcite you, make you tense, or distract you;
- the people and undertakings disrupting your capacity to create and maintain inner peace and order; and
- the submerged traumas stifling your inner fire and Sacred Tree.

The Spirit of Fire incites you to prioritize your inner peace and quietude by extracting yourself from distracting, disruptive, and/or abusive foods, substances, people, and/or situations. She encourages you to acknowledge suppressed suffering and offer love unconditionally to whatever part of you is sitting at the bottom of the well. She especially encourages you to speak up when you need to set healthy boundaries and implement wholesome self-care routines. She assures you that it is your birthright to be a peaceful, self-governing, and self-loving being.

The Spirit of Fire encourages you to sweep down to the warm earth to drink from her fire and reach to the sun with your branches. Hence, she lends you her calm vitality and joie de vivre!

HEART – DUODENUM – SMALL INTESTINE

SPIRIT OF FIRE
Physical Disharmony
15

You may tend to ignore your heart's guidance and song!

Whoops! You may be off-track, especially if the health of your biological heart, duodenum, and small intestine is wavering. You may have lost yourself in others, a cause, or just your day-to-day maelstrom of activities and perceived obligations. You may also be cut off from your heart's authentic voice. You may often say and act "Yes" when your heart says "No," or you may be inarticulate, hesitant, or shun opportunities to express your needs, beliefs, and opinions. Either way, your self-care and self-love curriculum may be sagging or disrupted.

Whether you aware of the impact or not, the Spirit of Fire encourages you to pause, reflect on these questions, and regroup.

- Are you often bubbling over with excitement or becoming excessively enthusiastic?
- Must you often be "on" and need to be the centre of attention?
- Are you often pushy, overly seductive, and/or aggressive verbally?
- Are you feeling more agitated, anxious, or more readily shocked?
- Are you often feeling overwhelmed by heartache, longing, and/or loneliness?
- Are you often dissociated more consistently or out-of-body?
- Do you often silence your authentic voice and truth?

If so, you may be trapped in a vicious cycle: disturbances in your heart, duodenum, and small intestine have adverse effects upon the emotional, mental, and spiritual aspects of your fire orb; and your emotional, mental, or spiritual disharmony impairs your heart, duodenum, and small intestine function.

The Spirit of Fire implores you to come back to basics! Set up a more wholesome routine, thereby cultivating a more loving and respectful relationship with your Sacred Tree. Self-care is nothing less than continuous self-love in action!

DISHARMONY STORY

You were raised in a Canadian-Italian family. Food is the big topic of conversation. When you gather, you endlessly eulogize the greatness of Italian cuisine. You all sit down to eat, and before you're finished this meal someone is already mapping out the next feast. As per usual, there is hell to pay. You feel like shit all night, and it takes you days to recover. You're so bloated sometimes that you look five months' pregnant, you're exhausted, you can't think your way out of a paper bag, and you're more likely to succumb to whatever bug is going around the office.

And you know this: the North American version of the traditional Mediterranean diet is more gluten-heavy. To make matters worse, North American wheat is more messed up. But food is your family's primary currency for expressing love. If you extract yourself from this exchange, you don't have much left. Besides, you often gravitate to breads and pasta anyway, especially if you feel like shit, because it's your "comfort food." Then, when everything goes to hell in a bread basket, you psych up and stick to a gluten-free program for a month, but by the time you're feeling shipshape, you're back at your mother's table again.

While the client's maternal mythology of irreproachable caregiving and love still resounds through the revered familial kitchen sounding something like this: "I prepare and feed you the most fabulous food in the world!," it also reverberates in the client's heart, duodenum, and small intestine. Unfortunately, the extraordinary food beyond reproach and promoted as the physical embodiment of love is harming the client's health and has since childhood. They often had belly aches, felt tired, and had a hard time concentrating in class and during homework. They also had panic attacks, and the contradiction reverberates in their familial relationships as well. Their father was volatile, controlling, and verbally abusive. Yet whatever storms blew through and still do, they all adhere to the familial myth of their magnanimous love, unity, and safety.

However, when the client's truth and heart song is suppressed, their duodenum, their trustworthy bullshit detector, jumps up and down and screams to high heaven. It's like clockwork. Sure, they had tummy aches as a child, but by the time they turned twelve, they had duodenal ulcers. Anyone who has experienced an imbalance in their duodenum will vouch that when something goes wrong, it hurts like bloody hell. Like the kidneys, its voice screeches. Their duodenum unfailingly makes it clear that what is coming down the pike is poisonous rather than nutritious, abuse rather than love. Furthermore, when the client's duodenum signals remain unheard and unaddressed, their heart's rhythm often summersaults into panic attacks.

Meanwhile, their small intestine whispers its flora imbalance more stealthily. Unfortunately, yeast overgrowth is often undiagnosed, yet it is virtually a pandemic. Wheat is an especially mangled crop in North America. Notably, it contains four times the amount of sugar than does European wheat. To make matters worse, the methods used to mass-produce flour and baked goods distort this grain and food beyond recognition. Although many wallets ignore the consequences, your gut speaks the truth. Your systemically poisoned digestive track and flora suffer immense consequences.

I work with children, teenagers, young adults, and adults who are collapsing due to eating wheat products in particular. The unmitigated and unconscionable mass production and distribution of enticing, addictive, and disease-causing toxins is often the smoking gun behind such imbalances as acne, psoriasis, fatigue, mood swings, headaches, foggy head, confusion, ADHD, depression including deep depression, chronic fatigue syndrome, candida, endometriosis (which I see as candida spilling outside the gut), and most autoimmune disorders, as well as most intestinal imbalances.

The Spirit of Fire incites you to prioritize your inner peace and quietude by extracting yourself from distracting, disruptive, and/or abusive foods, substances, people, and/or situations. She also encourages you to acknowledge suppressed suffering and to offer love unconditionally to whatever part of you is sitting at the bottom of the well.

HEART – DUODENUM – SMALL INTESTINE

SPIRIT OF FIRE

Emotional Harmony

16

The Spirit of Fire nurtures your "Yes" and urges you to share your truth!

16

When the Spirit of Fire's smile shines on you, your inner fire sparkles in her light. The heart of your Sacred Tree radiates inward and outward—you are wholeheartedly and joyfully manifesting your sacred relevance and in turn experiencing fulfillment and contentment. Thus ignited, the Spirit of Fire is broadening your Sacred Tree's capacity to receive and share peace, pleasure, and forgiveness in your day-to-day activities and relationships.

While radical self-inquiry and self-knowledge uphold your "Yes," it's radical self-love, self-acceptance, and self-forgiveness that unfurl your "Yes" into the world. The Spirit of Fire also teaches you to embrace others and their truth unconditionally. Hence, you build relationships based on respect and radical acceptance. You value honest communication and invest in its apprenticeship. You speak heart to heart. You face truth and convey truth. And if the Spirit of Fire invites your heart's voice to leave no stones unturned, you speak the secrets to dispel their charge and power over you. Remember, the Spirit of Fire assures you that you are never alone. She implores you to open up to the generous nectar of your trustworthy teachers, mentors, ancestors, angelic guides, spirit animals, and ascended masters.

The Spirit of Fire's enthusiasm and devotion harmonizes the fabric of your Sacred Tree with that of your partners, families, friends, local communities, and the global community.

HEART – DUODENUM – SMALL INTESTINE

SPIRIT OF FIRE

Explosive Emotional Disharmony

17

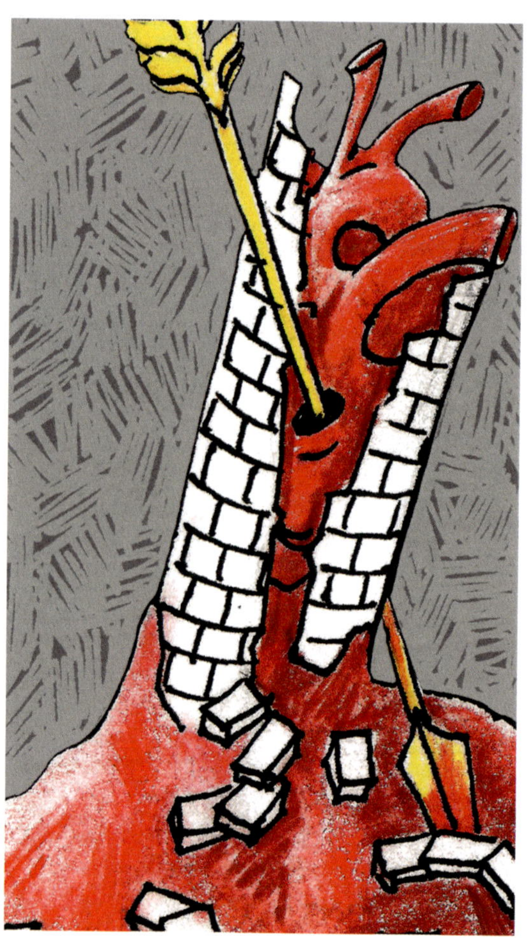

You may feel like a runaway train packed with explosives!

Take heart, as the soothing inner peace of the Spirit of Fire is accessible to you even now. The Spirit of Fire compassionately witnesses that you may be disoriented due to an excessive load of tumultuous and challenging events now or in your past. She encourages you to take stock of where you're at. Are you consistently showing up for yourself? Or, conversely, are you squashing your heart's voice?

- Do you consciously or unconsciously avoid acknowledging, recognizing, or understanding that you are abused or violated now or in the past?
- Are you consciously or unconsciously suppressing the recognition of the oppressor as the person you love?
- Are you creating a fantasy narrative that cleverly veils abusive events?
- Are you numbing out by becoming addicted to agitated mood states, for example, conflicts, risks, excitement, mania, arrogance, religious ecstasy, and/or sexual arousal?

The Spirit of Fire acknowledges that identifying abuse and abusive actions can be thorny and controversial, especially when you are hurt or you hurt others in the name of love. Often, people uphold their hurtful actions with the claim that "I'm doing this because I love you." The Spirit of Fire compassionately witnesses the intensity of your anxiety and agitation.

- You may be criticized, overmanaged, and/or colonized in the name of love or you do so to others.
- You may be disciplined, punished, and/or abused in the name of love or you do so to others.
- You may be oppressed, tyrannized, and/or enslaved in the name of love or you do so to others.

Whether you are deceived or you deceive others, the Spirit of Fire is with you. Her radiance will sustain you as you gradually navigate your way back to your inner fire, your innate wellspring of truth, peace, laughter, playfulness, and service.

DISHARMONY STORY

Your father has a steady job and a good income. He's a self-made man and built it all up despite poverty and childhood abuse. He pulled himself up by the boot straps and made something of himself. He's the solid foundation on which the household stands. Regardless, it's your mother's anthem: "He's the one we all depend on, isn't he?" And so the story goes. Yet he can be really scary. He flies off the handle, screams at the top of his lungs, makes all sorts of accusations, and even calls you names. The trail of reproaches he generates is endless: "You didn't help your mom make dinner again!", "You didn't do your dishes again!", "You didn't clean your room again!", "You didn't do your homework again!", "You slept in again!", "You were late for school again!", "You failed an exam again!" And on it goes.

The client is still so convinced that they're a lazy, stupid, crazy, and revolting good-for-nothing that they often consider ending their life. Although the client's father's usual tyranny of invectives is painful enough, one day we uncover a confrontation more terrifying than previously witnessed in other sessions. The client suddenly garbles through convulsive tears as they catch on to what I'm seeing. They now remember a specific time that they thought their father really had it in him to kill them because he was powerful enough, strong enough, mad enough, and menacing enough that day to really kill them.

Then, right on cue, their mother chimes in: "But he loves you very much! He bought you a bike, didn't he? He painted your room, didn't he? He drove hours to pick you up when you were stranded, didn't he? He really loves you! And all you do is spit in his face! You're nothing but an ungrateful, selfish little brat! You have no idea how much he loves you!" Whoa, he sure is dependable: on a good day, they can count on him to placate them; and on a bad day, they can count on him to shame them or scare the living daylights out of them!

When love is a wolf in disguise and all you know is contaminated love, you navigate the world with a totally screwed-up filing system with behaviour such as screaming, criticizing, lambasting, mocking, shaming, and berating in the love folder. Your heart wounds are then elusive and complex because beyond the straight-up and all too familiar stories of loss of love, absence of love, or betrayal, your heart is maimed by contaminated love. Untangling the multitude of ways in which love is distorted and polluted in a dysfunctional family or relationship is a long and subtle process.

Anodea Judith aptly describes this cyclical heartbreak in her seminal book *Eastern Body, Western Mind*: "Travesties of love occur when the most needed element of life is twisted and torn, withheld and used as a means of control. Without knowing what healthy love looks like, we have a hard time creating it in our lives. We hang on to the mere shreds of love, sacrifice ourselves on the altar, and run in fear when we find it. All forms of child abuse are, in fact, travesties of love. They are travesties because they are not complete nascence of love, but an absence of healthy love."

My heart spins to grasp the extent of the collateral damage over time. When you don't know love, love that is actually good for you, or you don't recognize contaminated love even when it bites you in the ass, you run the risk of being wounded again and again. You create relationships in your home, job, classroom, schoolyard, sports team, yoga studio, gym, yacht club, tennis club, restaurant, doughnut shop, pub, club, and even in your carpool without knowing what contentment, tranquility, and inner peace are or what respect, healthy boundaries, and joy feel like. It's a wonder some of us manage to stay alive despite hurtling down a hall of distorted mirrors at heartbreak speed!

The Spirit of Fire invites you to embrace your truth unconditionally and leave no stones unturned. She inspires you to name the skeletons in the closet and verbalize the fabricated love stories to dispel their charge and power over you! The Spirit of Fire assures you that you have the power to burn through the deception and repression!

HEART – DUODENUM – SMALL INTESTINE

SPIRIT OF FIRE
Implosive Emotional Disharmony
18

You may get lost in others and silence your truth!

Hey, where are you? The Spirit of Fire is calling on you! She sees you more clearly than you see yourself. It's come to pass that you know others' hearts more than your own and you honour their Sacred Trees more than your own. This upheaval at the heart of your being consistently disrupts your innate capacity to cultivate order, inner peace, and contentment. Whether sudden or gradual, this process has belittled your connection to your Sacred Tree, thereby causing you to live your life as a mere branch in search of a tree.

- You may get lost in others' feelings, needs, desires, life paths, and aspirations.
- You may expect others to prop you up to gain safety, stability, meaning, and/or happiness.
- You may implore others to rescue you and/or you attach to people fixated on rescuing or saving you.
- You may numb out by becoming addicted to "toxic" relationships that consistently generate heartache, longing, loneliness, self-sacrifice, and dissociation.

The Spirit of Fire also acknowledges that your truth may be silenced. Although you may bury your truth to escape from unbearable and overwhelming emotions, the silence nonetheless suppresses the heart of your Sacred Tree. The Spirit of Fire inspires you to snuggle with your not-so-warm-and-fuzzy past and animates your efforts to be honest with yourself and accept your truth unconditionally. She assures you that it's worth its weight in healing gold to explore the many ways in which you may deceive yourself and others.

- Do you trivialize your suffering by comparing it to the commonly recognized and publicized suffering of others?
- Do you whitewash experience by latching on to forgiveness too hastily?
- Is the true content of your experience swept away in the wake of traumatic severance and mourning?
- Do you publicly declare your love and devotion for someone often and may overstate their love, perfection, constancy, valour, or exploits?

Take heart, as the Spirit of Fire is with you. She gently yet assuredly cajoles you back to your own vigorous and mighty resource—your truth's density and your Sacred Tree's buoyancy.

DISHARMONY STORY

You are virtually incapacitated each week by unaccountable turmoil and pain, even though things are going really well on the surface. Your career is taking off after a successful debut. And longer term, you're not in that abusive relationship anymore; you have completed your undergraduate degree and graduate studies, and your dream of being a full-time artist is finally a reality. On the other hand, you are often in horrid pain; if not debilitating migraines, just about everything else. Anxiety crawls through you like ants, and explosive fits of grief and rage flatten everything in their wake. Fortunately, a helpful employer recommends you make an appointment with their chiropractor. You know nothing, but little by little he recognizes the pattern you present. He has treated many women with the same seemingly incongruous, helter-skelter rumblings.

One day, after a particularly intense release, I look into the chiropractor's eyes and see a version of me that I know he knows but I don't yet know myself. Yes, this is the story of the night when I, like many women who unexpectedly relive a memory of abuse, experienced the shattering of my world as I knew it. I suddenly remembered that my mother caught my grandfather with his fingers in my vagina when I was four years old. Although she hauled him out of the room at such a velocity that he barely touched the ground, she did not heave him out of our lives. My maternal grandmother sat helpless at the kitchen table, her eyes vacant and her trembling hands clenching a tissue; my father sat motionless as he always did when anything real was going down; and my mother yelled at everyone, including me. The sexual violation with this climactic family scene was, believe it or not, a normative performance. I gradually discovered, or rather recovered, the wretched truth that in my "family," sexual abuse was business as usual.

Like what?!? I thought I had everything a girl could want! My mother drilled my fortune into me: the pool, trendy bicycles, stuffed animals galore, luxurious meals in restaurants, beach holidays in Florida, private schools, figure skating, ballet, art classes! Apparently, you name it, I had it. The layers of confusion, denial, and dissociation never cease to amaze me. Over the years I also learned that my father's fast money also bought everything my mother wished for, including me: he was the dirty old john and my mother was my unscrupulous pimp. I spent years piecing together the whole sad lot. Hundreds of memories and years of abuse were stored in the cells of organs and tissues all over my body, but they had remained utterly inaccessible to my day-to-day consciousness until I was thirty-one year's old.

How can this be? It's now clear, for instance, that on days when my father intended to rape me, the menace in his eyes shot through me. It was like swallowing a Molotov cocktail. For years I had nightmares about this look alone, never mind everything else that occurred in the few minutes or hours that followed. My heart "broke" the instant my father's eyes told me our sacred father–daughter contract would be violated once more.

18

Ellen Bass and Laura Davis, the authors of *The Courage to Heal*, aptly point out that "Publicly acknowledged events are more likely to be remembered than events that are never discussed or are denied or ignored. Yet even sexual abuse which has public confirmation is more likely to be forgotten than an earthquake because of other factors, such as shame. There is no shame or stigma associated with an earthquake. If a person remembers being in an earthquake, it will not affect their sense of self-worth or self-esteem. She will not be blamed for the earthquake or told that she asked for it. And earthquake victims are not threatened with violent consequences if they talk about what happened."

It took more than ten years of therapy, meditation, and self-Reiki for my heart consciousness to trust that I could be present and remember some of the moments after that look without bursting into flames. Little by little I remembered that my father violently raped me when I was nine years old in the hockey locker room of the arena where I trained for figure skating; he raped me in his office on weekends more often than I can count; and he eventually drugged me, between the ages of thirteen and fifteen, so he could brutalize me for hours. My mother not only turned a blind eye but also took me to our "family doctor" with a stuffed brown envelope under her arm to pay for the illegal abortion that almost killed me at age fourteen.

From consciously apprehending and compiling NOTHING, other than apparently unaccountable emotional turmoil, I dove into the depths of my cells to reclaim my history, truth, and Sacred Tree. I lay with my now-conscious denial in the steaming tub for hours at least three times a week after seeing not only that chiropractor but a plethora of other body-focused healers, including craniosacral therapists, deep tissue massage therapists, Thai massage practitioners, osteopaths, and Reiki practitioners. They helped me to steer past my architect of survival, who had concealed the truth to survive, and to awaken my trustworthy body, which had stored the emotional maelstrom caused by sexual abuse, sexual servitude, and familial perfidy.

Your body's wisdom and a whole host of respectful inner and outer guides, including the Spirit of Fire, unfailingly escort you back to your Sacred Tree's harmony, tranquility, inner peace, and sacred relevance.

HEART – DUODENUM – SMALL INTESTINE

SPIRIT OF FIRE

Mental Harmony

19

The Spirit of Fire inspires you to make wise decisions, create order, and wield power with grace!

19

The Spirit of Fire, referred to as the Red Emperor in traditional Chinese medicine, encourages you to initiate radical teamwork with your elemental Spirits. Inner peace, tranquility, contentment, and fulfillment are the byproducts of concentration, receptivity, collaboration, and order. She encourages you to listen closely to all of your internal elemental advisers. The more often you lend an ear, the more often you will receive their guidance and insights. The more you reflect upon their teachings and regroup accordingly, the more you will receive the blessings of your innate healers:

- The Spirit of Wood's steering committee: love, compassion, kindness, patience, intuitive perception, and cognizance of your sacred relevance.
- The Spirit of Earth's solid foundation: trust, honesty, faith, openness, imagination, and your stable interconnectivity with Mother Earth and all living beings.
- The Spirit of Metal's social justice advocates: integrity, honour, dignity, and your generous capacity to engage in mindful and sustainable production and distribution.
- The Spirit of Water's wellspring of resiliency: wisdom, willpower, restfulness, and receptivity to ancestral and angelic guidance.

The Spirit of Fire also animates your desire to reach out to trustworthy teachers and elders to inspire and inform your meditative self-inquiry and actions. In turn, you also share your wisdom generously.

- You coach and impart knowledge joyfully.
- You present complex ideas in an accessible form.
- You are eloquent without being pedantic or plodding.
- You educate without pretention or self-importance.
- You love to unpack complex ideas with others.
- You encourage others to express their views.

When enchanted by the Spirit of Fire's radiance, you graciously recognize that your mind does not have all the answers.

HEART – DUODENUM – SMALL INTESTINE

SPIRIT OF FIRE

Explosive Mental Disharmony

20

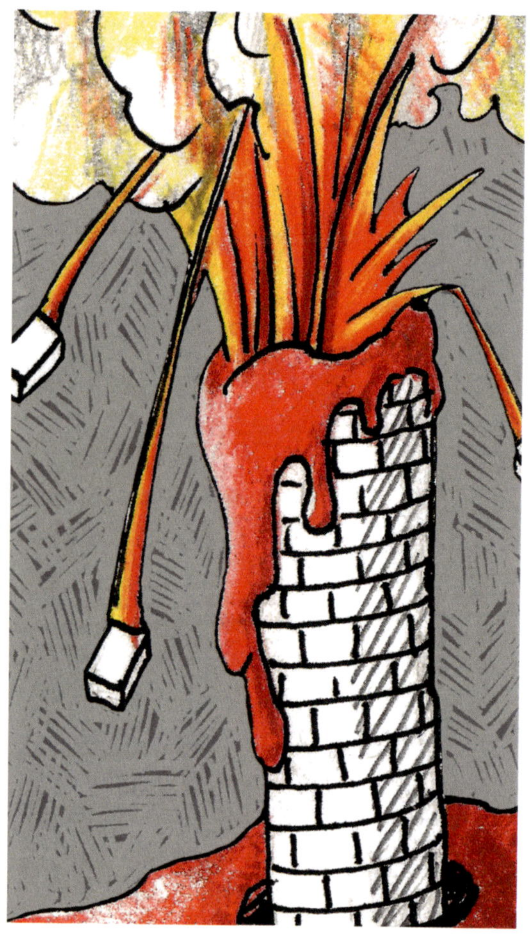

You may drown out your heart's wisdom and tranquility!

Whoa! Where are you going with that? Slow down! You need to take stock. Are you burying your emotional turmoil and discontent with excessive stimulation? Although the intensity may seem like a good way to avoid feeling and suffering, it's not ultimately serving you or your inner fire. At this rate, it's likely that you are suffocating the subtle music of your sacred relevance, thereby crushing your opportunity to receive the replenishing medicines of fulfillment and contentment. Before you know it, even your pilot light will be faint. The Spirit of Fire's soothing light signals that it's time to pause. She implores you to compassionately check in with yourself.

- Do you feel restless and crave intensity?
- Do you work most days and go out most nights?
- Do you seek extravagant stimulation and/or heart-thudding thrills?
- Are you compulsively belligerent, "bad," and/or rebellious to gain freedom, power, and/or control?
- Do you startle and shock others to shirk accountability and responsibility?

If so, you may be in reaction to the adversity in your past rather than anchored in your Sacred Tree and relevance. Regrettably, you're expending lots of energy in a conversation that leads nowhere you're going to like in the long run. The Spirit of Fire beseeches you to take stock, as this excessive and potentially hurtful energy may also express itself vocally. For instance, you may have a propensity to:

- be overly aggressive and/or dominate verbally;
- develop your debating and/or oratorical skills to assert and display your superiority;
- be overly witty, jokey, and/or a loudmouth;
- gossip or be a busybody; and
- be overly seductive verbally.

The Spirit of Fire snuggles in with you to assuage your suffering. Soften into her compassionate embrace and, when ready, call a council meeting with the Spirits of Wood, Earth, Metal, and Water. Welcome the opportunity to witness your innate Red Emperor in action, receive counsel, and gracefully regroup accordingly.

DISHARMONY STORY

Although you're not allowed to go out at night, you sneak out the window and go drink your face off anyway. Despite the fact that you must be a virgin until you marry, you make a point of fucking whoever you want. Even though you are now in your forties, it's pretty much the same routine, minus climbing out the window. While you sometimes yearn for a long-term relationship and you vaguely wanted a child a few years ago, you mostly enjoy your easy access to exciting-enough sex with your cast of fuck-buddies, party nights with friends, and, of course, your familiar ethyl alcohol buzz. You're riding it well enough: you still keep up with your full-time job and go out most nights, even though you're almost fifty. Yet lately something is off: you feel bloated, have a pesky yeast infection, and feel even more restless than usual. You seek opportunities to drink more often, jones for more intense sexual encounters, feel compelled to masturbate several times a day, and use pornography as often as you can.

To add to the excitement, the client is peri-menopausal! It's the last thing they want to hear, yet this beautiful built-in initiation and tenacious call to transform and evolve is knocking at their door. Although insistent rebellion and being a "bad girl" has been a lot of fun and still seems like a good idea, it has run its course for now. The client's fire organs are sending clear signals that this rebellious survival template is not serving them or their inner fire at this time. The commotion is drowning the subtle music of their heart and Sacred Tree, thereby stifling opportunities to cultivate and savour the Spirit of Fire's life-sustaining medicines: inner peace, order, fulfilment, and contentment.

I work with many peri-menopausal or menopausal women who suffer more consistently from candida and excess yeast-related symptoms—such as bloating, gas, constipation, brain fog, headaches, fatigue, dizziness, skin breakouts (not limited to face), sinusitis, allergies, or a weak immune system—than from the expected litany of symptoms linked to this hormonal transition. Their heart and gut are a reliable alarm system signalling to them that affairs of the heart need to be recalibrated to stay on track with their project evolution.

Thankfully, whether in peri-menopause or menopause or not, your duodenum and small intestine speak loud and clear if your house and heart are not in order! The heart in your gut reliably kicks up a fuss to ensure that you don't miss the opportunity to evolve. Furthermore, vaginal yeast discharge, an extension of candida in your gut, generally indicates that you need to take a serious look at your primary and sexual relationships, the more conventional matters of the heart. Vaginal yeast is usually a big fat "No!" to sex now, or with this partner, or with your multiple sexual partners, or whatever flavour of sex you are engaging in. These pesky physical symptoms are a sure sign that you're not listening to your heart's wisdom and aligning accordingly.

These symptoms are nothing other than a call to pause, reflect, assess, and clean house and heart. And if you're in peri-menopause or menopause, take heart: your wheels are falling off because it's time to upgrade to some serious treads because you need super cosmic traction for the most productive chapter in your life. What we conventionally refer to as menopause, the litany of uncomfortable symptoms and emotional turmoil, is a lot more than the sexist beacon of maligned deterioration. It is a sacred gateway and initiation as significant as the onset of menses. After mothering yourself and/or your children, you are now called to mother your communities. You are invited to step into your moccasins and join the healing circle of elders. In light of coming into service on a whole new level, it comes as no surprise that this call to transform is as clamorous as it needs to be to avoid being ignored, vilified, diminished, or dismissed.

The Spirit of Fire snuggles in with you to appease your agitation. Your heart, duodenum, and small intestine are steadfast guides helping you navigate an opportunity to evolve gracefully.

HEART – DUODENUM – SMALL INTESTINE

SPIRIT OF FIRE

Implosive Mental Disharmony

21

You may often say and act "Yes" when your heart says "No."

The Spirit of Fire's luminosity licks your inner fire awake at this time to help you recognize the substance of your Sacred Tree. She acknowledges that you may be disoriented and are conforming to other people's traditions, values, agendas, conditions, expectations, demands, and/or rules. She compassionately witnesses that you may be trapped in a good girl or boy mindset powerful enough to obscure your heart's song and sacred relevance. As a result, you may often be anxious, agitated, disorganized, unproductive, on the verge of panic, and/or experience panic attacks. The Spirit of Fire encourages you to pause, breathe, and reflect.

- Do you feel loved only when others perceive you as a worthy successor or trophy?
- Do you gain recognition from institutions that others respect?
- Do you pursue career paths that others respect to live up to their educational and/or financial aspirations?
- Do you seek love, safety, and validation from others by performing your duties with excessive fervour?
- Do you work so hard that you are often on the verge of panic or experience panic attacks?

Unfortunately, these distorted values encourage you to often say and act "Yes" when your heart and gut say "No!" Healthy boundaries and truthful communication are not only the stalwart guardians of your heart's desires, loves, and mandate, they are your birthright. Your Sacred Tree is not a rental; it's entirely yours to honour, protect, and defend. The Spirit of Fire entreats you to scrutinize when and why you say "Yes."

- Do you say "Yes" to be loved, to be safe, to please, to serve, to obey, and/or to appease?
- Do you say "Yes" to excessive, prescribed, frustrating, and/or draining expectations?
- Do you say "Yes" to destabilizing, belittling, humiliating, and/or degrading conditions?
- Do you say "Yes" to crazy-making, alarming, scary, and/or abusive obligations?

While radical self-inquiry and self-knowledge uphold your "Yes," the Spirit of Fire advocates that it's radical self-love, self-acceptance, and self-forgiveness that unfurls your "Yes" into the world.

DISHARMONY STORY

You consistently experience pain in your stomach at work. Your stools are often runny, and on really off days you have the runs. You commit to preparing and packing a gluten-free lunch instead of resorting to the food court every day. The pain reduces but creeps back in again and so does the diarrhea. You recognize that your anxiety steadily climbs throughout the day. You hope that leaving the building, breathing some fresh air, and walking for a half-hour will clear your head and reset your nervous system. It totally works. In fact, you even feel better on weekends because you're less cumulatively stressed out by the end of the week.

But slowly, feelings of discontent slink back in. You become more conscious that you're unhappy at work. More often than before, you dream of being an independent entrepreneur rather than a corporate CEO. Although your gut discomfort calms down for a few months, symptoms return with a vengeance after a particularly challenging week. You become acutely aware that the corporate culture, pressure, and lack of meaningful rewards are really getting to you. Yet you are on the verge of panic whenever you imagine life without the steady and sizable income.

You decide to add meditation to your morning ritual. Despite feeling calmer and clearer, your discomfort after eating is on the rise and your bowel movements are more acutely irregular and disruptive. You often have to leave the office early; and some days you don't make it in at all. Life, in general, is bleak. More than ever, you are aware that you have a noose around your neck; and although you're frustrated, your expenses keep escalating. You are increasingly ragged, and you have seen blood in your stools a few times.

Eventually your dis-ease escalates. You're barely keeping up with obligations, never mind the Joneses. Despite meditation and increased rest, your symptoms dramatically intensify, and you have to stay home for a few days. You finally drag yourself back to the office. By noon, you are in a cab to the hospital because there's suddenly a lot of blood in your stools. By sunset, you are an official emergency. To make matters worse, your blood pressure is dangerously high. By morning, you are diagnosed with a severe case of Crohn's disease and you are losing blood by the minute.

What does the client's small intestine, or more precisely their heart, want to hear? It wants a firm commitment that they will leave this job. While they sometimes experienced well-being, it was always temporary. Their meditation and walks did not totally mollify the impact of the soul-destroying grind of the corporate environment or compensate for how little their expensive lifestyle nourishes them. Their heart and gut are showing them that they are literally bleeding to death by not honouring their Sacred Tree.

Their heart is bawling and holding a gun to their head/heart, so to speak. There is no question: it is in their best interest to listen and take affirmative action immediately. I assure them that when they commit to quitting their job and changing their lifestyle, the bleeding will stop. In a moment of profound clarity and courage, they take the plunge and sign on the dotted line in their heart. They literally gasp when they make the commitment to make all the necessary changes to truly honour their sacred relevance. As anticipated, the bleeding stops within two hours.

Despite the client committing to this radical life-saving shift, thriving is months if not more than a year away for them. The cost to their health has been very real on all levels: physical, emotional, mental, and spiritual. There is no way around it, it's going to be a lengthy post-soul-destruction reconstruction program. It's unfortunate they waited so long to make changes, but it's never too late to set into motion a future with heart. Their heart and gut offered them a crash course in the value of paying attention when something is not working for them. They are learning to say "No" before their heart and gut have to say it for them. And they will learn this many times in small ways, and hopefully less dramatic ways, over the next few years.

Beware whenever your story or response starts or ends with "I have to" and "I should." I suggest you look long and hard for the travesty of the heart lying at the core of the chore, duty, responsibility, and/or obligation. More people do themselves in by uttering these falsehoods than all calamities deemed newsworthy. From where I sit, this mighty duo has caused more damage in the human race than all wars combined. The death toll, for sure, is greater. When you submit to other people's agendas and expectations despite your heart's advice, you undermine your Sacred Tree at a great cost. But rest assured, your devoted and loving body, your vehicle for your spirit in this lifetime, will not let it slide. It will say a big loud "No!" for you, and another, and another, until you listen, think, say, and act "No" when your heart says "No" and "Yes" when your heart says "Yes."

No one has the right to magnanimously set up expectations, rules, or dogma forcing you to ignore your heart's guidance. It can be anything from finishing the food on your plate, being the bookkeeper for your partner's company, inviting your sickly mother to move in with you, to staying in a job you hate or an unloving marriage. Following directives without questioning their relevance to you is a recipe for being systemically used and abused. If the person or activity creates heartache, longing, restlessness, overexcitement, nervousness, shock, anxiety, panic, or illness, then it's a clear signal that you need to create a healthy boundary.

Saying a hearty "No!" is often the loudest "Yes!" to love that you can utter.

HEART – DUODENUM – SMALL INTESTINE

SPIRIT OF FIRE

Spiritual Harmony

22

The Spirit of Fire inspires you to nurture yourself as well as others.

While your soul contract and sacred relevance is rooted in your liver and gallbladder, it's the laughter in your heart and gut that fosters the benevolent manifestation of your genius and service. The wholesome expression of the Spirit of Fire is the foundation of your sustainable yet magnanimous engagement.

22

- You compassionately and respectfully honour and nurture yourself and others.
- You enjoy your solitude and create wholesome relationships.
- You forgive yourself and forgive others.

Therefore, when your Spirit of Fire burns bright, you embrace yourself unconditionally and share your unconditionality with others. You respect who you are, fill your shoes, and respect others in theirs. Furthermore, when put to the test and a person hurts you, you know deep in your heart and gut that there is no guarantee that in their shoes you would have done differently; hence, you embrace radical forgiveness consistently.

Thus stoked, your inner fire also inspires you to speak from your heart authentically and thoughtfully.

- You stay fully present and reflect before you speak.
- You listen and create a safe space for others to be honest with you and open up.
- You nurture wholesome conversations without gossip and negativity.
- If called to leave no stones unturned, you speak truth to power or voice secrets to dispel their charge and power over you and/or others.

While your inner fire and its sacred relevance flow generously and joyously, the Spirit of Fire imparts her gentle yet hearty medicines of peace, order, fulfillment, and contentment with you and all living beings.

HEART – DUODENUM – SMALL INTESTINE

SPIRIT OF FIRE
Explosive Spiritual Disharmony
23

You may tend to chase highs!

Ouch—it's super hot! The Spirit of Fire beseeches you to put on the brakes. Slow down without delay to compassionately witness the intensity and frenzy of your drive, striving, or cravings. Your motivations and enthusiasm may be blistering hot and potentially scorching you and others. What was once enticingly spicy and radically healing may now regrettably injure your Sacred Tree ecology rather than inspire sustainable healing and growth in alignment with your sacred relevance. The Spirit of Fire encourages you to take a deep breath, pause, and soften into compassionate self-inquiry. She fosters your capacity to acknowledge the possibility that you may be seduced by a very alluring and magnificent commotion—spiritual bypassing.

- Do you use meditation to avoid your emotions and traumatic past?
- Do you confuse dissociation with true equanimity?
- Do you focus on the intellectual and studious aspects of spiritual practice and therefore live in your mind rather than in your heart?
- Do you crave and seek big spiritual fireworks?
- Do you pursue rituals with powerful medicines in highly charged contexts?
- Do you seek exhilarating romantic soul-to-soul love?

The Spirit of Fire is very familiar with this seductive delusion and recognizes its allure and escalating hazards. If the high winds persist, the fire can go out of control: you may elevate and separate yourself from others, self-aggrandize with spiritual Technicolor wow-ness, and/or hide behind grandiose spiritual prowess.

- You may make efforts to always be "on" and be the centre of attention.
- You may speak of your personal opinion and beliefs as the only truth and proclaim the superiority of these beliefs.
- You may proselytize and be preachy and/or long-winded.
- You may tenaciously defend or adamantly argue the righteousness of your beliefs.

The Spirit of Fire encourages you to embrace yourself unconditionally and share your unconditionality with others. She nurtures a more easeful and mindful spiritual exploration capable of generating a magnanimous yet sustainable engagement with all living beings.

DISHARMONY STORY

You are drawn to working with powerful sacred medicines and psychoactive plants in a variety of contexts. You live in a large urban centre and travel a lot. You enjoy endless opportunities to join sacred ceremonies, ecstatic dance circles, and festivals such as Burning Man. Some are less formal than others, and some aren't formal at all, but no matter. You are passionate about exploring the sizable menu of options on a number of continents. You are proud of navigating with relative ease these intense and thrilling group ceremonies, including self-directed medicine journeys. Your colleagues, clients, lovers, and friends look to you as a spiritual seeker and adventurer of considerable proficiency and appeal. You're known for the scope of your inspiration and enthusiasm whether you're at a clinic, seminar, workshop, retreat centre, yoga class, community event, or dance circle. Your practice is booming, and your workshops are well-attended.

All is well, sort of. While the client gravitates to heart-opening journeys and tends to focus on spiritual growth, they also tend to get carried away, especially when they're settled for a few months in a foreign location. Although their bi-annual quest tends to start off as a healing journey, gentle enough to keep track of their insights and slow enough to work through to the manifestation of these insights on the earth plane, within a couple months they tend to tumble into a more compulsive back-to-back solo-journeying mania.

On the one hand, they take advantage of being sturdier than most physically to withstand the disruption of their sleep and the serial physical, emotional, mental, and spiritual purging several times a week. On the other hand, the upheaval consistently catches up with them. By the end of their quest, rather than being more peaceful, replenished, and fulfilled, they habitually become more restless, agitated, and anxious. The benefits from their more tender and heart-healing rituals early on are habitually hijacked by the thumping excess of repeated all-night group ceremonies or solo medicinal plant explorations. What starts off as an opening into the magnitude and divinity of the self escalates into an escape from the self. It's easy these days to be seduced by the alluring muddle of spiritual bypassing.

Regrettably, the enticingly spicy and radically healing potential of the medicinal ceremonies also escalates into a feeding frenzy building up way too much heat. The client's wholesome spiritual motivation is also usurped by excessive striving and cravings for spiritual fireworks. They end up damaging their Sacred Tree ecology rather than cultivating sustainable healing and growth in alignment with their sacred relevance. The Spirit of Fire encourages you to take a deep breath, pause, and soften into compassionate self-inquiry without medicinal plants also. It's important to strike a balance. Trust the capacity of your Sacred Tree's wholesome fire to sustain high enough levels of concentration to push all doors open.

23

The Spirit of Fire encourages you to calmly burrow your roots deep into the earth and reach for the sun with your branches. Your fire's tender song licks awake every cell of your Sacred Tree and infuses you with the gentle cadence and magic of your sacred relevance. Don't underestimate the innate alchemical power of your Sacred Tree's wholesome fire to transcend all of your limitations.

HEART – DUODENUM – SMALL INTESTINE

SPIRIT OF FIRE

Implosive Spiritual Disharmony

24

You may be self-sacrificing to a fault!

The Spirit of Fire reaches out to all of you overly dedicated and selfless caregivers, parents, activists, social architects, and spiritual seekers. The formidable vortex of self-sacrifice has a long patriarchal history; hence, the intensified risks for women, who can more easily fall prey to this age-old imbalance of power suppressing rather than nurturing their Sacred Trees. That said, it's a menace for all genders, especially if you tend to focus almost exclusively on the well-being of others and/or are devoted to a familial, cultural, political, or spiritual organization or faith. The Spirit of Fire beseeches you to pause and reflect on the backbone of your initiative and drive.

- Do you self-sacrifice to be worthy of love?
- Do you self-sacrifice to be worthy of esteem?
- Do you self-sacrifice to be worthy of enlightenment?
- Do you tend to be inarticulate, hesitant, or shun opportunities to express your needs, beliefs, and opinions?
- Do you lie or silence your voice to be loved, approved of, and/or validated?

You can imagine that if these conditions escalate, you're not going anywhere pretty. The Spirit of Fire recognizes that you may be at risk of being exploited or abused and that a sexist dynamic may significantly escalate the imbalance of power and danger. The Spirit of Fire is here to shed light on a potentially sensitive and charged situation.

- Does your elders', leaders', teachers', or faith's political and organizational infrastructure, beliefs, conventions, rules, practices, and/or rituals undermine your self-worth, personal authority, power, and freedom?
- Do you submit and defer to their opinions, authority, mastery, intellectual knowledge, and/or psychic prowess?
- Do you steer clear of honest and truthful conversations, circumvent direct questions, and/or dodge opportunities to speak truthfully?
- Does your elders', leaders', teachers', or faith's political and organizational infrastructure, beliefs, conventions, rules, rituals, and/or practices systemically oppress, torment, shame, and/or belittle you?
- Are you confined in a crusade or cult and controlled by its founder or leader?

The Spirit of Fire inspires you to nurture yourself and others, and most importantly forgive yourself and others. Laughter in your heart reliably fosters the benevolent manifestation of your genius and sacred relevance.

DISHARMONY STORY

You're only fifty-five years old, but you've already had several bouts of cancer, including breast cancer twice, and now you have cancerous lesions in a few spots along your spine. You've had chemo many times, radiation twice, and travelled to developing countries to get treatments and go on cleanses not yet legal in Canada. Some of it worked; you're still alive, after all. But this time your health is declining more rapidly and you feel like you don't have much fight left in you. You're exhausted all the time and have lost your special knack of being on top of everything.

I place my hands on the client's body and the core of their chakras are strikingly clogged. I go on to find a spiritual teacher in their root chakra at the base of their spine blocking their connection to the earth; he's in their second chakra too, interfering with the seat of their kundalini energy; he's in their third chakra undermining their self-worth; of course he's in their heart, for they love him way more than they love themself; he's in their throat chakra thwarting their voice and personal authority; he's in their sixth chakra thwarting their intuitive perception; and lastly, he is in their crown chakra shading the sun. It's a complete takeover. The cancer lesions in their spine correlate with the thwarted chakras perfectly. Unfortunately, their condition speaks of their immense devotion and constancy, yet it tragically broadcasts their self-sacrifice and self-neglect.

Sadly, their confusion is unsurprising. First, like so many other devotees, they thought they had to go through their guru to access high vibrations rather than connect to the earth and the sun directly. Second, they interpreted selfless service to be self-sacrificing service. Contrary to a widespread confusion, selfless service is actually the manifestation of your sacred relevance emerging directly from your Sacred Tree rather than self-sacrificing actions performed solely for the benefit of others. The wholesome manifestation of your sacred relevance always nourishes you and all living beings simultaneously. Hence, your heart fire transcends the effort of service sustainably and generously.

Third, the train wreck does not stop here. They also spent years devoted to their children and spouse. It's been self-sacrifice all the way. As for being a self-sacrificing mom, there's no surprise there either, motherhood has been distorted for centuries by sexist doctrines. It's a legendary sinkhole. Contrary to popular and sexist opinion, motherhood is not synonymous with self-sacrifice. Self-sacrificing motherhood is basically a compulsory and willful disregard of your rights, feelings, needs, desires, and sacred relevance for the benefit of your spouse and children. Regrettably, this falsehood serves the patriarch rather well.

This neglectful list describes nothing other than the systemic oppression of women. If a mother's heart and love is so immense, then surely there's enough juice in there for the mom.

Sacrifice is a renunciation, and self-sacrifice is nothing less. Besides, if you fail to celebrate your Sacred Tree, how can you be an efficient channel for love? How can love live in you, through you, and with you? How can you create joy for your children if you do not know, taste, and revel in joy also? Yet the client was expected to, and routinely expected herself to, generously love everyone, yet at the core of her life and being, she institutionalized scarcity and oppression. That ship has royally sunk too many times to count.

The Spirit of Fire beseeches you to respectfully honour and nurture yourself and others, enjoy your solitude, create wholesome relationships, and forgive yourself and others. She revels in the wholesome and sustainable manifestation of your sacred relevance and basks in your heart's laughter.

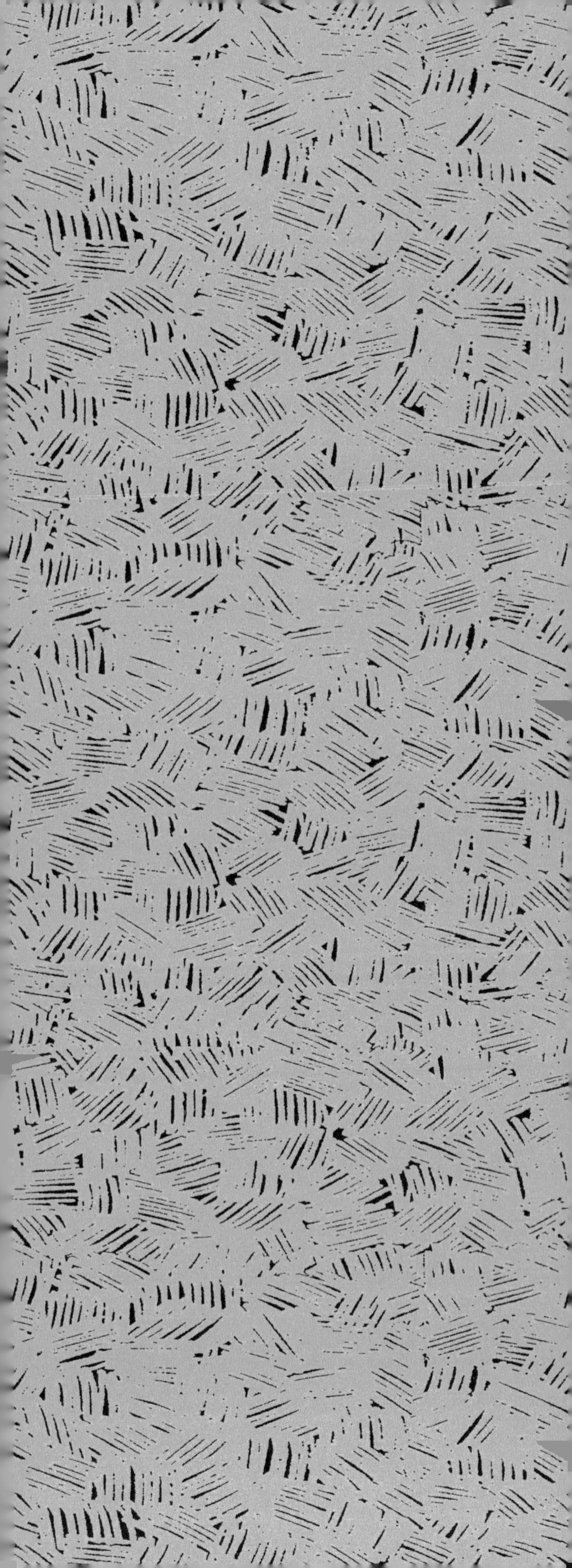

CHAPTER 5

SPIRIT OF EARTH

土 SPIRIT OF EARTH

COLOUR	SEASON	YIN ORGANS	YANG ORGAN	EXTERNAL ORGAN
Yellow	Late Summer	Spleen Pancreas	Stomach	Mouth

EARTH ATTRIBUTES	LATE SUMMER PULSE
Stability, Clarity, and Strength Unconditional Nurturing of Earth Body Vitality and Revitalization Interdependence with All Living Beings, including the Earth	Burrow your roots in the earth. Eat fresh foods to heal your earth body. Mindfully manifest your service. Hang out in Nature and receive her guidance.

HARMONY	EXPLOSIVE DISHARMONY	IMPLOSIVE DISHARMONY
HIGH-VIBRATION EMOTIONS	EXPLOSIVE LOW-VIBRATION EMOTIONS	IMPLOSIVE LOW-VIBRATION EMOTIONS
Trust Honesty Faith Openness Imagination Stability	Abandonment Obsessiveness Workaholism Competition Covetousness Instability	Worry Regret Self-Doubt Remorse Suspicion Diversion

EARTH	HARMONY	DISHARMONY
PHYSICAL	**26** You are grateful for your physical body's wisdom and generosity. You have faith in its competence and self-healing prowess. You readily open to its counsel and act on its guidance. You eat well, rest well, and sleep well.	**27** You may experience spleen, pancreas, and/or stomach ailments. You may demand too much of your body or neglect it. You may be overactive or underactive; you may overeat or undereat; you may overperform or underperform.

EARTH	HARMONY	EXPLOSIVE DISHARMONY	IMPLOSIVE DISHARMONY
EMOTIONAL	**28** You are robust and resilient and bend in the wind rather than snap or be uprooted. You trust yourself and trust the earth. You surround yourself with trustworthy people who support the development of your creativity and life path.	**29** You may feel unworthy and alone in the world. You may feel abandoned, rejected, vilified, and/or censured. You may be destabilized by a human-centric personal, economic, and geopolitical narrative.	**30** You may be perilously busy. You may perform excessive chores and/or work overtime without adequate support or recognition. Others' expectations may drain you. You may suppress your emotions and numb yourself with activity.
MENTAL	**31** You dedicate an adequate amount of time and energy to your intellectual, creative, activism ventures, and outdoor adventures. You work and nurture yourself simultaneously. Sustainability is a built-in prerequisite.	**32** Your authentic inspiration and imagination may be hijacked by your quest to gain external validation, financial rewards, or prominence. You may push to get ahead rather than nurture your genius and service.	**33** You may inhabit manufactured realities and fantasies more vividly than your own. You may indiscriminately consume fantasies and information on social media, the Internet, TV, and in movies. You may hunger for the ideals portrayed.
SPIRITUAL	**34** You trust the earth and the sun, and in turn you are trustworthy and transcend geopolitical borders. You invite her teachings through your bare feet. You foster your and others' enthusiasm, curiosity, creativity, imagination, and playfulness.	**35** Others or/and their cultures may interfere with the development of your spirituality, intellectual capacity, creativity, and/or imagination. You may be starved spiritually, intellectually, creatively, and imaginatively.	**36** You may be tragically cut off from the earth and the sun. Your screensaver may know the earth's natural wonders more than you do. You may be starved for time off in Nature. You may underestimate the power of rooting in the earth.

SPLEEN – PANCREAS – STOMACH – MOUTH

SPIRIT OF EARTH

Sacred Tree in Late Summer

25

The Spirit of Earth spurs you into a timely self-healing of your foundation!

25

While the warm and glowing light of the Spirit of Earth in late summer wraps you in her loving arms, you undergo your last burst of external growth before the autumn and winter. She beckons you, Sacred Tree in modernity, to soften into her belly to savour her ancient, life-sustaining potency. She entreats you to burrow your roots deep into her stabilizing and motherly embrace to soak up the copious nutrients at her breast.

More than anything else, your roots embody your interdependence with all living beings, including the Spirit of Earth. After all, it's to your roots where your sap retreats in winter to dedicate time and energy to self-inquiry and contemplation. Hence, the Spirit of Earth teaches you that your roots are your reliable and sacred refuge to receive guidance on how to revitalize your life force and sacred relevance. In that sense, the roots of your Sacred Tree caress intimately the source of all life and sustainable and meaningful action.

Furthermore, the Spirit of Earth tantalizes you into healing your earth body with a plethora of invigorating fruits and vegetables ready for the picking. She encourages you to change up your food program, to go beyond maintenance mode, and get on track with a focused and curative reinvigoration effort. She lovingly urges you to capitalize on the bountiful energy of late summer to shore up your Sacred Tree and fill the larder with beautiful life-sustaining preserves for the winter months ahead—when the pantry is full, you can thrive through the winter by circumventing scarcity and depletion or the fear of scarcity and depletion.

The Spirit of Earth implores you to firmly anchor into her body and take the time to absorb her life-sustaining nourishment, especially in times of growth, change, and transformation. Hence, she relishes the opportunity to support you in those few weeks between seasons when autumn changes to winter, winter to spring, and spring to summer and holds you up during high winds, turmoil, and adversity. When you neglect fastening your Sacred Tree securely to the Spirit of Earth, you may weaken and risk toppling in times of drought or storm. Therefore, when in doubt, remember the Spirit of Earth and burrow into her committed and vigorous embrace.

The Spirit of Earth forewarns that the principle of abundance and decrease is at play. Eat well, revitalize, and heal now. You will need this foundation and resource in the months ahead.

SPLEEN – PANCREAS – STOMACH – MOUTH

SPIRIT OF EARTH

Physical Harmony

26

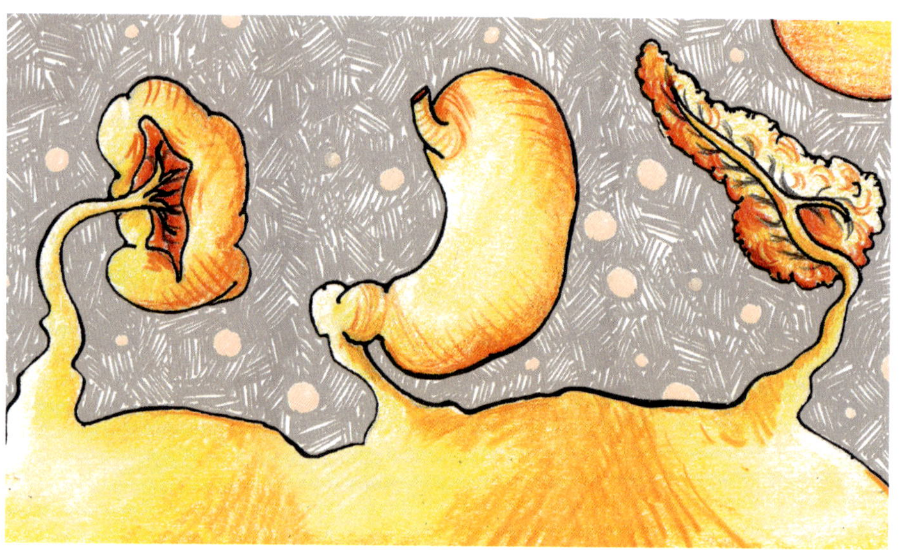

The Spirit of Earth inspires you to accept your body's invitation to co-operate!

The Spirit of Earth prompts you to delightfully root your spirit in your physical vehicle in this lifetime. Be grateful for your physical body's wisdom and generosity. Have faith in its competence and self-healing prowess. Readily open to its counsel and act on its guidance. And most importantly, remember that you are one with the great Earth Mother. Respect your interconnection with all living beings. Welcome the earth's heartbeat and healing vibrations and let them inform your rhythm and impulses.

- Eat well, exercise, and self-heal. Go beyond maintenance mode and get on track with a focused and curative reinvigoration effort while being mindful of your body's shifting needs in various seasons, circumstances, and ages.
- Relax, rest well, and self-heal. Restorative yoga and Yoga Nidra offer an immense body of knowledge on the art of healing by resting constructively. Practise Savasana, the corpse pose, the quintessential practice of receiving. Remembering how to receive and absorb beneficial vibrations is nothing less than the active undoing of the contraction of survival.
- Sleep enough and self-heal. Sleep is a very complex experience, much more so than wakefulness. Give yourself enough time to delve into the mysterious wonder of this profound opportunity to recalibrate. It is a supreme gift you can offer yourself daily.

Your earth body is your Sacred Tree's foundation and your most trustworthy ally.
Step it up and show up for the basics: eat, rest, and sleep.
Sustain self-healing long enough to energize your evolution.

SPLEEN – PANCREAS – STOMACH – MOUTH

SPIRIT OF EARTH
Physical Disharmony
27

You may neglect or abuse your earth body!

The Spirit of Earth calls you to her: "Come back, child! I haven't felt your feet on my belly in a long, long time. Interweave your roots and earth body with mine. My love, blessings, and nutritious resources lie in store for you." The Spirit of Earth is tenderly reminding you of your earth body's interdependence with hers and all living beings. The health of your Scared Tree relies on your interactive, vital, and respectful relationship with Nature. Trust her, it's definitely not a long-distance relationship and you're not going far sustainably without her or a healthy earth body. She is Mama, after all! She is signalling that it is essential for you to burrow your roots into her and replenish your stores, especially if you are experiencing growth, changes, and/or ailments of the spleen, pancreas, and/or stomach.

- You may be perilously stagnant, sedentary, and indoors most of the time. You may sit for hours each day, barely leave your screen, and/or rarely exercise.
- You may be precariously overactive—working long hours indoors and trying to accomplish an endless to-do list.
- You may socialize a lot despite fatigue, focus on competitive goals, and/or exercise excessively.
- You may be systemically malnourished due to inadequate prioritizing, misinformation, the omnipresent distribution of junk food, and/or lack of fresh fruit or vegetables due to geographical constraints or poverty or both.
- You may repress your hunger and eat inadequately or eat excessively and compensate for overeating by excessive exercise, purging, fasting, and/or forced vomiting and extreme use of laxatives, diuretics, enemas, or colonics.
- You may suffer from institutionalized malnutrition due to misinformed guidelines, high profit margins, or systemic oppression in class-informed and/or race-informed schools, health and military institutions, seniors homes, or the prison industrial complex.
- People may use food, or the lack thereof, as a means to control, oppress, torture, or degrade you.

The Spirit of Earth encourages you to rejoice in Nature; eat, relax, and sleep; and get on track with a focused and curative reinvigoration effort. She lovingly urges you to capitalize on her bountiful energy to shore up your Sacred Tree and fill the larder with beautiful life-sustaining preserves.

DISHARMONY STORY

You are driven to excel and compete in mountain biking. You adhere to a rigid and vigorous training schedule despite your professional commitments, relationship, and children. You push yourself to reach greater levels of fitness, competence, and competitive performance despite mounting anxiety. Although the pressure to achieve your goals creates the high you crave, you fret about your merit all the time and experience debilitating trepidation and self-doubt.

Your intense agenda leaves little time for rest, romance, and playful exploration. In fact, you barely have time to think, never mind thrive. Despite the thrill of accomplishment and triumph you experience when you reach a goal, your joy is fleeting. Increasingly, a gnawing feeling of emptiness overwhelms you when you are alone. In these moments, you binge on carbs and sweets. Sadly, this numbing relief is short-lived, amplifying your insecurity and self-loathing. You then resort to vomiting, something you are even more ashamed of. In fact, no one knows about it. You are tormented by this devastating secret cycle. It's clear to you that your health and marriage are suffering, and you worry yourself sick about the impact on your children.

The level of anxiety in the client's body was striking, yet when asked about their upbringing, they smiled nostalgically and proclaimed they had a happy childhood. Yet I sensed that the sizzling anxiety, pressure, and eating disorder was much older than their passion for mountain biking, or their career, marriage, or children. It turns out that their birth family was into sports, and it was expected that both children compete fiercely and triumph in gymnastics. The client even hailed their mother's ardent interest as a fervent vote of confidence and love.

However, when we pulled back the curtain, we discovered that their mother neglected her children's need for additional rest during growth spurts, aching muscles, injuries, digestive disturbances, colds, flus, headaches, and illnesses. Their training schedule did, perforce, override their emotional upsets too. In fact, the intensity of the gymnastics training and the rigid diet to maintain the lean body deemed essential to excel was so strict that both sisters only started their periods in their twenties.

Although the daily grind was daunting for both sisters, the client had to work extra hard to keep up with their more advanced and successful older sister. Their mother's insistent and sometimes threatening directives to do their best were a constant reminder that love could be withheld if they didn't equal their sister's proficiency. Unfortunately, this additional strain fostered many opportunities for traumatizing embarrassment, shame, and public humiliation. The threat of rejection and dejection was real and ominous daily.

The client spent their childhood and teenage years running ahead of a pack of scary wolves—humiliation is no hatchling. Their mother's obsessive expectations not only gave rise to anxiety, self-doubt, uncertainty, and low self-worth but also fostered a profound spiritual disorientation. The non-negotiable focus on athletic prowess smothered the client's connection to their innate Sacred Tree. While athletic performance became their currency to earn self-respect and external validation, it smothered their imagination, interests, dreams, and non-athletic genius. Who are they really? What is their sacred relevance? If a child, teenager, or adult does not have time to explore, discover, and follow their curiosity, their uniqueness and sacred relevance remain untapped. The consequences are tragic! When self-worth and self-knowledge is not firmly rooted in their Sacred Tree, they are cut off from their birthright to express outwardly and manifest from a deep-rooted connection with their unique sacred relevance and medicine. Their gift is lost on them and on all of us!

Have faith in your self-healing prowess, especially if you're strung out, tired, and depleted. Open to your earth body's counsel and act on its foremost guidance before going any further with anything: stop, hang out in Nature, and rest!

SPLEEN – PANCREAS – STOMACH – MOUTH

SPIRIT OF EARTH

Emotional Harmony

28

The Spirit of Earth motivates you to stand on your own two feet!

The Spirit of Earth is not just a backdrop to your human drama, whatever it is. You know her intimately and trust your teacher and mother. Therefore, you are consistently present in your earth body and feel anchored, safe, and robust yet resilient—you bend in the wind rather than snap or be uprooted. You are also open, self-confident, self-disciplined, productive, empathetic, and honest, managing your resources and hers with respect, mirth, and wonder. After all, there are mountains to inspire you, trees to guide you, lakes cool enough to make you squeal, and there are docks to rock you to sleep!

Together with Mother Earth, you create a lavish yet sustainable, personal, and communal ecology. Although you enjoy collaboration and appreciate companionship and leadership, you remain self-reliant and retain your connection to your own imagination and inspiration. You surround yourself with nurturing and trustworthy people who:

- buoy your dreams;
- foster curiosity;
- nurture your creativity and imagination;
- encourage free-form fantasy; and
- respect your sacred relevance.

When you are rooted in the Spirit of Earth and her forests, you thrive within the enchanted community of her ancient and sacred trees.

SPLEEN – PANCREAS – STOMACH – MOUTH

SPIRIT OF EARTH

Explosive Emotional Disharmony

29

You may feel unworthy and alone in the world!

Yikes! Your creativity, concentration, and productivity may be hijacked by worry, trepidation, self-doubt, anxiety, panic, and/or post-traumatic stress. It's huge! The Spirit of Earth compassionately witnesses that you may be experiencing abandonment, neglect, and/or ostracization or that you do so to others. Whether it's in your family, community, office, faith, and/or geopolitical context, you may be declared unlovable, unfit, and/or objectionable or you do so to others. Regrettably, the charge may be so disruptive that you feel frantic and uprooted.

The Spirit of Earth reassures you that she is right here with you. She is nothing less than your primary caregiver and embraces you unconditionally. Therefore, she is not only your protector, trustworthy ally, and refuge, she is your teacher. She assures you that no matter who these people are who deny you your sense of belonging or safety, you are first and foremost her child and can always turn to her for love, nourishment, support, and insights. The Spirit of Earth recognizes that you may be in the grip of an overly human-centric narrative.

- You may be more intensely destabilized because you are overly fixated on another human being as your anchor and safety net.
- You may be perennially depleted because you believe that you are your only source of subsistence and sustenance.
- You may be swept up by a torrent of misgivings because you may be overly captivated, impressed, or obsessed with an infamous human controller, manager, and exploiter of the earth's resources and other living beings.
- You may latch on to an unreliable public figure or someone very familiar and be perennially dumbfounded by their incapacity to meet your community's foundational needs to feel safe, secure, nourished, and supported.

The Spirit of Earth forewarns that you may be rejected, censured, or vilified because you are independent, free-thinking, and therefore threatening to a status quo that needs to be toppled. Trust the power of your sacred relevance and stay the course.

DISHARMONY STORY

You've been overwhelmed and tormented by unremitting worry, anxiety, and self-doubt for decades. Although you exercised compulsively, dieted mercilessly, and tried hard to concentrate in school and university, you still obsess with your "failure" to be as attractive, thin, and smart as other students. Later, when you created a beautiful home, prepared healthy meals, and did whatever was needed to ensure that your partner and children had everything they needed, it was never perfect enough either. Moreover, when you try to please your mother and still submit to her will, she does nothing but dominate and exploit you further. You feel unworthy of love and respect no matter where you turn. Besides, you're losing it! You are strangled by devastating migraines, debilitating loneliness, and post-traumatic stress.

It's a relentless treadmill at best! As per usual in sessions, the plot eventually gets past the intensity of the turmoil on the surface. We eventually discover that the client was often molested by a domestic attendant around the ages of five and six. When they reached out to their mother for protection and reassurance and told her what was happening, their mother flew off the handle, accusing them of being responsible for making it happen. Rather than gather their child up in her arms to ascertain their wounds and soothe their physical and emotional pain, she spit out words such as *slut* and *whore*. The day this victim of repeated sexual violation spoke up is the day they were brutally rejected and abandoned by their mother! The cascade of distress, turmoil, and shame quickly mutated into profound shock. To this day, their mother misses no opportunity to remind them that they are an undeserving and tainted child—nothing they do is right or good enough to erase the stigma of sexual abuse.

Although the client is exiled from their mother's heart, they are indelibly shackled to each other. While their mother still has to endure this curse-of-a-child she birthed (?!?), the client still needs and craves their mother's love and approval. Unfortunately, this debilitating cycle is not confined to this relationship or childhood, adolescence, or young adulthood. Systemic oppression and powerlessness have dictated most of the client's roles, including employee, partner, and parent. Fortunately, after years of therapy and self-care they are untethering the steel cables of intergenerational sexism, cultural biases, and abuse. Their muzzled truth and repressed trauma are breaking free and so are the migraines!

29

You are a magnificent Sacred Tree
rooted in the Spirit of Earth!
You are as beautiful and worthy as every
other human being. You have the birthright
to be a self-governing, empowered,
and relevant human being. You exist,
and you count, and you matter!

SPLEEN – PANCREAS – STOMACH – MOUTH

SPIRIT OF EARTH

Implosive Emotional Disharmony

30

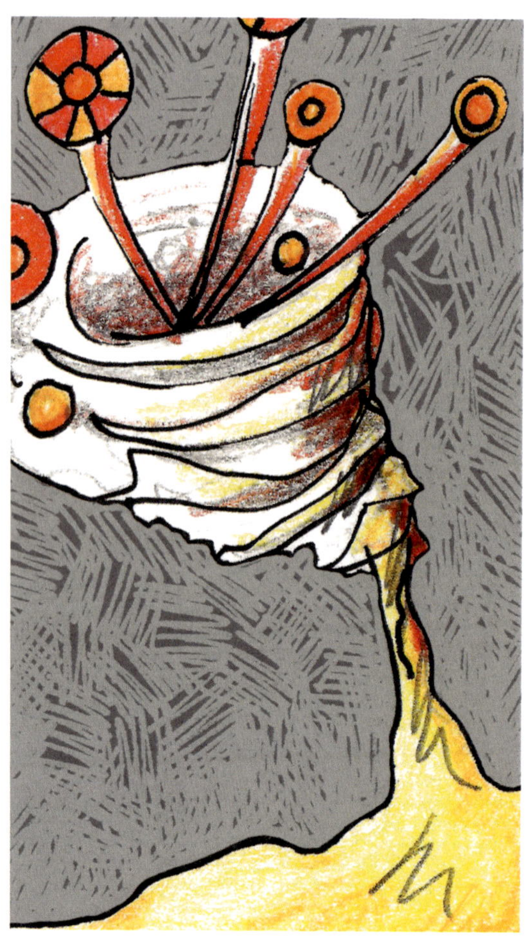

You may be perilously busy!

Geez Louise, you are one busy human being! No matter how urgent, persuasive, captivating, compulsive, or addictive your activities are in the short-term, the Spirit of Earth presages that you may be courting burnout or a life-threatening or debilitating disease in the long-term.

First, the maelstrom of activity may encroach on your freedom and leave you without time to heal, develop your intellect and creativity, and/or pursue your dreams.

- You may perform excessive chores, work overtime a lot, and/or work late into the night and on weekends a lot without adequate support, recognition, and/or financial reward.
- Others may expect you to be responsible for your partner, children, parents, and/or family business without adequate support, recognition, and/or financial reward.

Second, you may avoid tuning in to your feelings or numb yourself by compulsively pursuing activity, busy work, and/or distractions.

- You may be addicted to work, hobbies, sports, worship, committees, TV, Internet, fitness, health, sex, cleaning, organizing, shopping, gambling, and/or "endless" education.
- You may use your intellectual pursuits, political causes, and/or artistic dedication to drown out unresolved pain and suppress your emotions.

The chicken or the egg? Super tricky and endlessly convincing either way! The Spirit of Earth compassionately witnesses that you are in an unsustainable muddle bound to leave you worked up, hollow, and depleted.

The Spirit of Earth urges you to pause, clear the decks, and get yourself to Nature somehow. She offers you her mountains and valleys, oceans and streams, and the wisdom and vivacity of all living beings, including your own anchored and robust Sacred Tree!

DISHARMONY STORY

You're stressed out and exhausted. No surprise there, as you're working really hard to succeed in your studies, budding career, and relationship. Truth be told, you push really hard, obsess, and work yourself to the bone at everything you do. On your good days, you're dedicated and inspired; on your bad days, you tend to be freaked out, distrustful, and controlling. You're gnawed at by the persistent feeling that it's never really going to happen for you—your right to thrive feels mysteriously threatened. You push hard to express, succeed, and shine. You soar sometimes, but it always withers—something always gets in the way. Furthermore, your vitality and energy tend to spike and crash a lot. To your dismay, you now have diabetes. You're on meds and it all seems under control—still, it's crushing to be in this predicament.

While it's old news that the client's parents divorced when the client was ten years old, we soon discover they comforted their mother when she was reeling from the unanticipated divorce—her husband had suddenly pulled the earth out from under their gingerbread house when he announced he was involved with another woman. Their mother tumbled into a heap of despair and powerlessness, and she lashed out against her now-reviled ex-husband and his new partner.

This young ten-year-old galvanized whatever resources they had to soothe their mother and pitch in with chores to keep what was left of the gingerbread house afloat. Even though their mother's frailty was frightening and overwhelming, they rallied, worked hard, and took care of their little brother. Despite being fearful of losing their father forever, they nursed their distressed mother. Hence, at ten years old, they lost their mother too—they were now mothering her! Unfortunately, their subjective experience was buried under their mother's tidal wave. They, too, were panicked, bereft, helpless, and despairing, but their suffering took second place in the unfolding drama.

Therefore, abandonment and bitterness lay under the ten year old's brisk and helpful productivity. "Dad is gone!" "Is it forever?" "Am I going to be allowed to see him again?" "How often?" Where?" "Mom hates him!" "She hates her!" "I love him!" "I like that woman. She's nice." "I miss him!" "Like, what the hell?" "What about me?" "Who is taking care of me?" "Who cares about me?" "What about my life?" Their panic, apprehension, resentment, rage, fear, confusion, sorrow, and even love could not be expressed freely, especially their emerging tenderness for the other woman and their happier, more relaxed dad.

30

At age ten, their gingerbread childhood was irrevocably a thing of the past; the present was out of their control; and their future appeared to be in jeopardy. Triple OUCH to their Spirit of Earth, pancreas included. Deep within, they knew they needed a guardian and mentor to evolve. Just when their sense of self was burgeoning, they got thrown perilously into a world governed by adult chaos and perfidy. "Does anybody care about my gift?" "How will my gift grow?" "How can I possibly do it alone?" "My life is ruined!" "I'll never blossom." "I'll never get to do what I am meant to do." "It's ALL derailed!" Without their caregivers' roots strengthening the Spirit of Earth and home, they feared that their Sacred Tree and sacred relevance were perennially threatened.

Thankfully, none of this is written on the client's being in permanent ink, even though it feels like it. The client eventually rekindles their relationship with their innate Spirit of Earth and learns to trust the power and magnificence of their Sacred Tree. They now more consistently experience the Spirit of Earth meeting their feet when they step into their genius and relevance. They thrive rather than survive!

The Spirit of Earth encourages you to create a sustainable personal and communal ecology. While you enjoy collaboration, you remain self-reliant and retain your connection to your own imagination and inspiration.
You surround yourself with trustworthy people who buoy your dreams, nurture your creativity, and respect your sacred relevance.

SPLEEN – PANCREAS – STOMACH – MOUTH

SPIRIT OF EARTH

Mental Harmony

31

The Spirit of Earth inspires your intellect, creativity, and imagination!

31

In counsel with the Spirit of Earth, you nourish your body–mind–spirit, thereby creating a solid foundation for expansive investigation and assimilation of subtle and complex discoveries. Your mindful and embodied presence is the foundation of your intellectual framework, artwork, or platform for social change.

- You engage in mindful activities, insightful production, and service.
- You are vibrant and have the ability to study and think clearly.
- While you are discerning, precise, and intellectually rigorous, you remain open to exploring new ideas and intuitive insights.

Furthermore, the Spirit of Earth forewarns that it is essential that your authentic inner philosopher, intellectual explorer, spiritual seeker, counter-culture artist, and/or renegade activist remain in good hands. Hence, she renews your commitment to sustainability as a built-in prerequisite not only in terms of ethical viability, truthfulness, and honesty but also in terms of wholesome stamina and productivity.

- You need to dedicate enough time and energy to your intellectual, creative, and activism ventures as well as your outdoor adventures.
- You need to nurture yourself and experience ease, comfort, and flow despite extended periods of work.
- You need to strike a balance between pushing to get things done and healthful work habits.

The Spirit of Earth celebrates your wholesome and healing bond with your earth body, and continually prompts you to support your genius with mindful work habits to sustain joyful manifestation.

SPLEEN – PANCREAS – STOMACH – MOUTH

SPIRIT OF EARTH

Explosive Mental Disharmony

32

Your authentic inspiration and imagination may be hijacked!

Oops, your productivity may be derailing! You may be pushing ahead rather than nurturing your genius and sacred relevance. Although you may gain financial security, influence, and/or prominence, you may be perilously disoriented and escalate your expectations despite feeling uninspired, muddled, stressed out, and/or dissatisfied. The Spirit of Earth compassionately witnesses your ungrounded exertion and strain.

- You may seek others' validation and approval to the detriment of your fulfillment, internal compass, and imagination.
- You may work longer and longer hours to compete, win again, and/or climb echelons despite weariness, anxiety, and/or lack of inspiration.
- You may join as many committees, boards, and/or agencies as possible to gain influence, accolades, and prominence despite being disenchanted and cynical.

Unfortunately, your quest for prestige, prominence, triumph, and/or financial reward may smother your inspiration, creativity, and imagination. You may have lost your true north! For instance, your cause, passion, and sacred relevance may be eclipsed by your quest to produce quantity versus thoughtful quality; or the fickleness and grandiosity of the star system in academic, artistic, activism, or other professional cultures may distort your goals, discernment, political discrimination, truthfulness, and/or honesty.

The Spirit of Earth calls you back to your foundation. Slow down and take a break in Nature—you need time and space to rekindle your connection to your essence and Sacred Tree to become genuinely inspired again!

DISHARMONY STORY

You're successful and settled. You have tenure at a reputable university, you love your students and your partner (on good days), you have two great kids, a house, a yard, two cars, a dog, and you're totally stressed out and exhausted. "Anything could go wrong, right? It could all fall apart, right? I could lose my job, right? I could get really sick, right?" It's relentless. You are hunted down by this pack of scary thoughts virtually every night. You actually wake up with a jolt, sit bolt upright, and live through the very real impression that everything could and will collapse. Night after night, you sit in the dark, helpless and gasping at the horrifying prospect of catastrophe.

Distrust, worry, and insecurity are not new to the client. When we explore their childhood, we quickly run up against their capable, successful, and patriarchal father and his exacting agenda. He prioritized scholarly and academic success above all else. He expected them to ace it in all subjects and imposed an additional workload to amplify their intellectual prowess in spelling, grammar, and science. They were pressured to compete in spelling bees, driven to become the leader of the debating team, and pushed into becoming the victorious class president.

Regardless of the achievements they garnered, more always loomed on the horizon. He bombarded them with insistent and sometimes threatening demands such as "You have to get A's" or "You have to be the best." Their play time and free time, perforce, were truncated to a minimum. He punished or shamed them when they did not apply themself or succeed enough. Unfortunately, the threat of rejection and the menace of becoming a "silly woman like their mother" looms over the client still! Silly woman like their mother?!? Yikes!

Although the client thrives in a noteworthy and reputable academic career, they are tormented by the risk of failure "by womanhood," so to speak. Their gender works against them—of course it does; institutions are still riddled with sexism and there is no shortage of proof to this effect in the client's student and professorial career. Hence, the underlying belief that they are flawed and must compensate is internalized and unconsciously governs their choices and priorities: they focus more and more on financial rewards and prominence; they take on too many graduate students; they numb their feelings; and they don't take time off.

The cycle of violence is alive and well. While their male colleagues enforce the same regimen and prejudice that their patriarchal father imposed on them, the internalization of the sexist mindset persistently bypasses their impassioned feminist education and awareness. The unresolved trauma feeds their urgent climb in a male-dominated hierarchy and their determination to buttress their pride with accomplishments recognized by male colleagues. Unfortunately, their frantic persistence weakens their stability, openness, trust, imagination, intuitive intelligence, and alignment with their sacred relevance.

The cycle can end, and it does. Gradually, they loosen the grip of the architect of survival propelling them to excel academically to be rewarded, respected, and loved by their father and other patriarchal figures. They more consistently take the time to rest, eat well, hang out in Nature, and spend quality time with their partner and kids. They also take the time they need to explore and regroup professionally.

The Spirit of Earth inspires you to nourish your body, mind, and spirit to create a solid foundation for expansive investigation and assimilation of subtle and complex discoveries. Your mindful and embodied partnership with the Spirit of Earth is the underpinning of your intellectual framework, artwork, and/or platform for social change.

SPLEEN – PANCREAS – STOMACH – MOUTH

SPIRIT OF EARTH

Implosive Mental Disharmony

33

You may inhabit imaginary worlds more vividly than your own!

Damn it, you may indiscriminately consume profit-driven fantasies, information, and/or news/reports on the Internet, social media, television, and/or Netflix/Amazon and the like! The Spirit of Earth compassionately witnesses that your concentration is most likely capsized by these sensationalized fictional and/or non-fictional human-centric narratives, romance, sex, extravagance, tragedy, and/or brutality.

33

- You may be fascinated, fanatical, and/or addicted to television series, animation series, video games, and/or pornography.
- You may be riveted by the excitement, drama, and/or intensity of the characters' storylines more than by real people.
- You may be captivated by a character's manufactured beauty and swagger or have crushes on the characters and/or stars.
- You may be thrilled by a character's power over others, ferocity, and/or violence.

Consequently, you may be too flooded with embellished and distorted stimuli to focus on creative and meaningful activities and relationships. Sadly, you may also equip your children with media-controlled technologies and unwittingly encourage them to be engrossed in distorted and misleading values and ethics.

- You and/or your children may be overly preoccupied with your and others' "imperfect" bodies, weight, hair, complexion, clothing, and wrinkles.
- You and/or your children may hunger for a "perfect" body, fireworks romance, trophy sex, and/or pornography.
- You and/or your children may consciously or unconsciously emulate power-over dynamics influenced by overt or covert heterosexist, sexist, racist, and/or ethnocentric content.

The Spirit of Earth implores you to turn off your screens and run to Nature for a cleansing reboot at the life-and-love buffet. The wisdom of trees and all living beings in loving action awaits you!

DISHARMONY STORY

You're stressed out and numb all the time. Your partner keeps bouncing off your fog bank and frequently "wigging out." You know it's affecting your kid too. You're down on everything and check out most of the time. You are plugged into Netflix, get stoned a lot, and drink too much. You're also the master of procrastination: your freelance work suffers and you're not pulling your weight financially either. It's all on the line. The whole thing could collapse any minute. Your partner is at the end of their rope and so are you. You're miserable!

When I lay my hands on the client, I perceive a huge rift in their world when they were in their early teens. "Oh yeah! My parents got divorced when I was twelve." "What was that like?" I ask. "Well, my dad was MIA for months on end, my mom was a mess—she was a nervous wreck. Yeah ... it was rough. My sister spun out of control—she partied all weekend, was out at all hours, and started skipping school. Mom was worried sick about her." "What about you?" I ask. "Me? Oh ... I was fine. School was boring, I played lots of video games, watched TV ... hung out in my room ... You know, normal teenage stuff."

"Fine? Holy cow! Wait a minute, let's backtrack here. I sense tremendous shock. I don't think you were fine at all." The client is unaware they were in shock too and expressed it very differently than their mother and sister. They were actually perilously fixated on video games and television, cultivating a long list of fictional families and friends rather than fulfilling relationships. They were tweening alone in their bedroom! By the time they were fourteen, fifteen, they turned inward even more and masturbated a lot rather than meet and explore their sexual awakening with other teenagers. Gradually, they masturbated more and more compulsively, not so much to feel but to stop feeling. Eventually, they discovered they could numb out even more when they watched porn online. The more obsessively they masturbated to porn, the more dissociated they became.

They not only lost their father that fateful day, but they lost their mother and sister too. Nothing and no one was ever the same after that. Their suppressed feelings and unresolved abandonment trauma has been festering and sinks deeper into their being by the day. The vicious downward spiral due to dissociation and old architects of survival, who served for a time but no longer contribute to their life, is crushing. Of course, their marriage and parenting are suffering! They continue to fill the gaping chasm with social media and Internet porn, as well as junk food, recreational drugs, and whatever they can put their hands on to continue numbing and suppressing.

33

Once the client connects the dots, they are immediately on board with the love-and-compassion program. They get to know their tween, love him to bits, and become their own trustworthy caregiver. They compassionately witness the self trapped in a secret corner fuelled by porn and a sprawling fog bank of weed and Netflix and gently offer them respect rather than scorn. Their new understanding ignites kindness, and with it they open doors that worry, remorse, self-doubt, and low self-worth had sealed shut. Showing up with love also steadily dispersed the smothering loneliness and isolation. They actively self-healed their shock and trauma, gradually dismantling the architect of survival's need for those unwholesome strategies. It's never too late to reach a disoriented younger self!

The Spirit of Earth encourages you to nourish your body-mind-spirit by spending time in Nature to restore and renew your Sacred Tree-ness. Your curiosity, enthusiasm, and capacity to transform will soon rouse from their slumber and disorientation.

SPLEEN – PANCREAS – STOMACH – MOUTH

SPIRIT OF EARTH

Spiritual Harmony

34

The Spirit of Earth inspires you to trust her and in turn you are trustworthy!

34

The Spirit of Earth cajoles you into firmly rooting into her. She inspires you to wholeheartedly celebrate your earth body with spiritual practices such as meditation, devotional chanting, activities in Nature, movement to join body–mind–spirit, and/or cleansing. The more you invite her teachings through your bare feet, the more she stimulates your enthusiasm and curiosity. Hence, the joy of discovery bolsters the development of your creativity and imagination, which in turn sparks the ecstatic manifestation of your dreams and sacred relevance.

The Spirit of Earth teaches you how to live with her and all living beings rather than attempting to control, manage, or exploit yourself and/or others. She encourages you to be accountable vis-à-vis yourself, other living beings, and the planet. It's impossible to think of a tree without presupposing the presence of the Spirit of Earth or the complex interdependent ecology that supports it. Therefore, you transcend geopolitical borders, including villages, cities, countries, nations, and continents. You regale in the magnificence of the earth and all living beings no matter where you are, what activity you participate in, or what tribe you contribute to.

*You enthusiastically absorb and integrate the Spirit of Earth's genius and wisdom,
and in turn you offer yours to all living beings, including her.*

SPLEEN – PANCREAS – STOMACH – MOUTH

SPIRIT OF EARTH

Explosive Spiritual Disharmony

35

Others or their cultures interfere with the development of your creativity and imagination!

Watch out—you may be starved spiritually, creatively, and imaginatively! The Spirit of Earth compassionately witnesses that your opportunities to open up to the world, its wonders, and the people in it may be smothered. Tragically, your birthright to independently dream, contemplate, explore, imagine, create, play, and manifest may be obstructed.

- Your activities, creative ventures, thoughtful inquiry, scrutiny, and/or truthfulness may be overtly or covertly censored.
- Your imagination may be asphyxiated by prepackaged ideals for your body, home, career, interests, and aspirations.
- Your innate openness may be hijacked by the dominant culture's pragmatic cynicism and suspicion.
- Your dreams may be usurped by preordained generalizations, qualifications, quantifications, and classifications.

Consequently, your initiative and confidence may be corroded by the dominant culture's spin on what's attractive and repulsive—desirable or undesirable. Your endeavours, interests, hobbies, hopes, and/or dreams may be criticized or discredited. Increasingly, you may underestimate your genius and minimize the magnitude of your sacred relevance and service. In the end, you may even undervalue creativity, exploration, intellectual inquiry, observation, and/or unstructured play.

The Spirit of Earth beseeches you to plunge your roots deep into her core. Together, you will restore your connection to your Sacred Tree and relevance.

DISHARMONY STORY

Your looks garnered enough flattery and praise to sweep you off your feet by age ten. In your mid-teens, the perks fuelled a whirlwind of sexual encounters and thrills. By your late teens, you were virtually airborne on its magic carpet ride of bonuses, including prominence, covetous attention, exuberance, nightclubs, sex, ethyl alcohol, and some E and the like thrown in for good measure. Your early and mid-twenties were a throbbing cocaine blur, and you were consumed by a whirlwind of attraction and conquests at work and at play. By age twenty-eight, you have already been repeatedly burned romantically, sexually, and professionally. You are perilously disoriented and feel "fucked up" and "fucked over."

The client was granted the treacherous *beauty passport*, a channel to privileges handed out to those who fit the beauty ideals of a particular era and fashion. Fortunately, though, the transformational power of their first Saturn return shed light on its duplicity. Our Saturn returns (at ages twenty-eight, fifty-six, and eighty-four approximately) are momentous openings of a spiritual portal when the planet Saturn completes an orbit around the sun and returns to the same zodiac sign it was in when you were born. The first Saturn return, which unfolds between the ages of twenty-seven and thirty, is a spiritual rite of passage rekindling your connection to your Sacred Tree. Saturn, the whistleblowing taskmaster of the skies, bolts in to highlight the disharmonies and blockages interfering with your sacred relevance. It insists you wise up, make judicious choices, and recognize that your genius is more than skin-deep. The more perilously distracted, stubborn, or unplugged you are, the more daunting the process and invitation tends to be. Although you may slither away and hide from it for a few years, there is no getting away from it entirely. You're relevant enough, even if you don't yet realize the far-reaching implications of your worth and unique genius.

This built-in initiation and call to transform precipitated the client's bewilderment, exhaustion, misery, and disillusionment. It's unfortunate, but all privilege passports are intoxicating and the complex cultural and geopolitical snares are formidable. Thankfully, the aphrodisiac cacophony of illusory power came crashing down. The power and privilege was never in their hands; it's the boys and men who had the power all along. Unfortunately, their conspicuous physical "assets" increased the relentlessness of systemic sexist socialization and fortified the internalization of the male gaze.

Although their physical beauty was a currency that earned a lot of validation and attention, the built-in sexism robbed them of personal power, personal authority, self-respect, and worthiness. Often they loved themself only when their physical beauty was rhapsodized. Hence, the sexist lens stared back at them every time they looked in the mirror. Their need to retain beauty, and with it their *beauty passport*, created anxiety, trepidation, insecurity, and self-doubt. In addition, the dizzying maelstrom of this passport distracted them. They lost touch with their Sacred Tree and squandered their ingenuity. Their innate Sacred Tree, along with Saturn's call to attention, sounded the alarm loud enough for them to slow down enough to do some therapy, take time off from sex and relationships, lay the foundation for a self-care program, and within a year or so catch up with their Sacred Tree enough to be a more astute and trustworthy gardener and caretaker.

The Spirit of Earth forewarns that the only passport worth having is the one you have from the get-go: your innate Sacred Tree, which predates the gender story, race story, nuclear family story, national identity story, culture story, fiscal wealth and safety story, and all other fabricated privilege stories.

SPLEEN – PANCREAS – STOMACH – MOUTH

SPIRIT OF EARTH

Implosive Spiritual Disharmony

36

Your screensaver may know the earth's natural wonders more than you do!

36

Holy moly! Whether you know it or not, you are starved for Nature's beauty and wisdom big-time! The Spirit of Earth recognizes that you may be so caught up in a human-centric plot that you have lost track of Nature's mystic and foundational intelligence and abundance. The Spirit of Earth compassionately witnesses that your disconnect and distraction is likely reinforced by the dominant culture and the systemic disorientation of human beings around the globe. Hence, you may neglect to check in with Nature's knowledge, and your perception of the world and your place in it may have become hierarchical, oblivious, and/or disrespectful. The Spirit of Earth calls you back to the fore to remember the sagacity of Nature's elemental building blocks shared by all living beings, including animals, plants, and rocks.

- You may live in a large city amid relentless concrete, asphalt, and pollution and travel to other cities almost exclusively.
- You may have grown up in a city and were not given the opportunity to experience enough free play and exploration time in Nature.
- You may spend an inordinate amount of time indoors.
- Your urban and/or indoor routine may not include enough Nature interludes/adventures in local parks, beaches, gardens, and/or rural environments.
- You may fail to prioritize Nature and travel expenses in your household budget.
- If you do plan a trek, adventure, or respite in Nature, something usually gets in the way and you cancel.

The Spirit of Earth forewarns that no matter where you think you're heading and what your priorities are, your respectful and active engagement with all living beings is essential, life-giving, and life-sustaining. Nature is not a backdrop to your life—it is your life.

DISHARMONY STORY

You work a lot and spend most of your waking hours at the office. You are the backbone of your company and do whatever it takes. You, perforce, think ahead, revise the company's mandate, do research, enlarge your web presence, generate promotional material, envisage new markets, and upgrade your office's technology to keep up with industry standards. Plus, there's always another looming deadline, an unexpected challenge, or a new and improved expansion plan. Besides, you have to be there to pick up the slack, ensure deadlines are met, compensate for incompetence or negligence, or save the day if someone happens to drop the ball! "It's for real!"

It's all heart-thumping real: the hazard of inaccuracies, blunders, and slip-ups; the risk of letdowns, flops, and failures; the threat of decline, slumps, or a market crash. It's all-consuming and insular. So much so that the client has no idea that there really is a whole world out there. When the maelstrom of your life takes precedence over Nature, the heartbeat of the Spirit of Earth becomes smothered. Your metronome, your hormones, are going to go haywire relatively quickly. It's guaranteed: your physical body will deplete, your emotional body will become turbulent, your mental body will become turbid, and your spiritual body will collapse in on itself. Then where are you going? It's impossible to think of a tree without presupposing the presence of the earth and the sun. We are no different. Divorcing yourself from Nature is no less destructive than uprooting a tree and throwing it in an office. No matter what you're up to, you need to be with the Spirit of Earth so that, in turn, the earth is with you. No matter where you think you're heading, this foundation is essential, life-giving, and life-sustaining.

36

Pause,
when you're about to say
no to a walk in the park,
when you're about to say there's
no time to go swimming,
when you're about to say there's too
much traffic to go to a cottage,
or when you're about to say you can't
possibly go on a
Nature trip this year.
Pause, and think it through again.

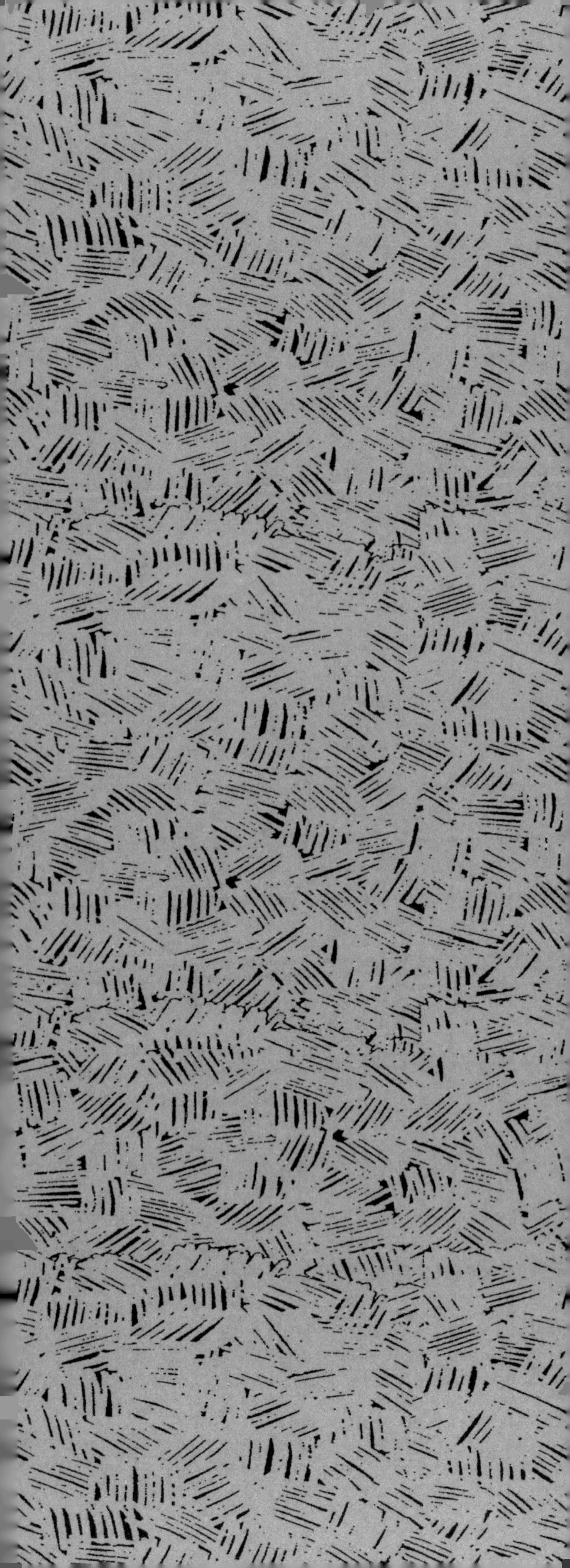

CHAPTER SIX

SPIRIT OF METAL

SPIRIT OF METAL

COLOUR	SEASON	YIN ORGAN	YANG ORGAN	EXTERNAL ORGAN
White	Autumn	Lungs	Colon	Nose

METAL ATTRIBUTES	AUTUMN PULSE
Dignity and Self-Worth Recognition of Value Beyond Yourself Global Consciousness and Social Responsibility Generosity Letting Go and Shedding	Open up to your essence and love. Savour the fruits of your hard work. Distribute what you have produced. Sort, consolidate, and purge. Prepare for winter and do not overexert.

HARMONY	EXPLOSIVE DISHARMONY	IMPLOSIVE DISHARMONY
HIGH-VIBRATION EMOTIONS	EXPLOSIVE LOW-VIBRATION EMOTIONS	IMPLOSIVE LOW-VIBRATION EMOTIONS
Integrity Honour Justice Dignity Generosity Social Responsibility	Excess Grief Guilt Greed Control Affluence Exploitation	Shame Sorrow Disappointment Stinginess Self-Pity Pessimism

EARTH	HARMONY	DISHARMONY	
PHYSICAL	**38** You accept change and aging. You do not participate in the corporate proliferation of products or therapies, exploiting your or others' fear of aging. Your fluid breath is a conscious exchange with all living beings.	**39** You may experience lung or colon ailments. Your sense of self and your place in the world may be shaky or rigid. You may feel stuck or unyielding. You may swallow your feelings.	
EARTH	**HARMONY**	**EXPLOSIVE DISHARMONY**	**IMPLOSIVE DISHARMONY**
EMOTIONAL	**40** You greet grief and soften into its inevitability. You embrace beginnings and endings, death and rebirth. You appreciate the magnitude and payback potential of change and transformation.	**41** You may have lost your moorings. You may be inconsolable, morose, exhausted, and/or apathetic. You may evade grief and potential disappointments. You may never cry.	**42** You may be tormented by shame and/or humiliation. You may feel inferior, tainted, scorned, and/or reprehensible. Shame may suffocate your dignity, self-worth, and/or accountability
MENTAL	**43** You capitalize on your genius for the betterment of the world. You focus on mindful and ethical objectives, production, and distribution. Profits do not influence or distort your genius, objectives, and service.	**44** You may define your self-worth with your job, house, lifestyle, or material gain. You may tend to be jealous and covetous. You may prioritize accumulation over relevance and service.	**45** Scarcity and fiscal concerns may smother your aspirations, genius, and service. Your genius may be cut off from the "air" it needs to thrive and serve. You may remain in thankless or abusive jobs.
SPIRITUAL	**46** The earth's and the sun's abundance flow into the world via your committed and dynamic materialization of your genius and service. You transcend prevailing and imperious commerce with creativity, insight, and grace.	**47** Your desire to dominate and generate personal profit may be out of control. You may push to preserve or increase your gains, surplus, or hegemony even when they endanger other living beings.	**48** You may be trapped in the vault of the economy, a human-made construct based on a capitalist and a colonialist framework. You may take what is precious and take it for yourself.

LUNGS – COLON – NOSE

SPIRIT OF METAL

Sacred Tree in Autumn

37

The Spirit of Metal buttresses your dignity and generosity!

The chilliness of autumn ends the sap in your trunk and branches downward to your roots in preparation for winter. Your foliage dries and withers and eventually flutters to the earth in her brisk cool winds, thereby granting you a vision of who you are in your essence. Hence, the Spirit of Metal reinforces your sense of self-worth and dignity and assures you that your innate genius and service is a wellspring of sacred medicine and life-affirming nutrients. It's harvest time, after all! The Spirit of Metal urges you to be grateful and savour your Sacred Tree's delicious fruit and that of others.

The Spirit of Metal also encourages you to recognize the might of a wholesome in-and-out flow and, conversely, the negative impact of attachment and accumulation. She coaxes you into letting go of your leaves so they may decompose and enrich the soil, thereby nourishing and strengthening Nature's regenerative cycle. Therefore, she fortifies your capacity to respect not only yourself but also what lies beyond yourself. She buttresses your sense of justice and integrity and bolsters your global consciousness, social engagement, and generosity. She urges you to distribute and share with all living beings what you have produced fairly and generously.

The Spirit of Metal also prods you to let go of what is not necessary or detrimental. She assists you in identifying what is precious and necessary and teaches you to eliminate anything stale, unnecessary, or harmful. The Spirit of Metal reminds that there is no point in holding on to your leaves in case you need them next year! It's time to make room for new people and experiences to help you learn, grow, and evolve.

Furthermore, the Spirit of Metal cautions you not to overexert. As Nature moves into a period of rest, you are reminded that the time for "putting it all out there," the summer, has passed. It's time to cultivate your body–mind–spirit connection, be more introspective, and learn to exercise your will more quietly and calmly. It's a good idea to finish up projects and enjoy the results of your hard work.

The Spirit of Metal inspires you to soften, respect, receive, let go, and share.

LUNGS – COLON – NOSE

SPIRIT OF METAL

Physical Harmony

38

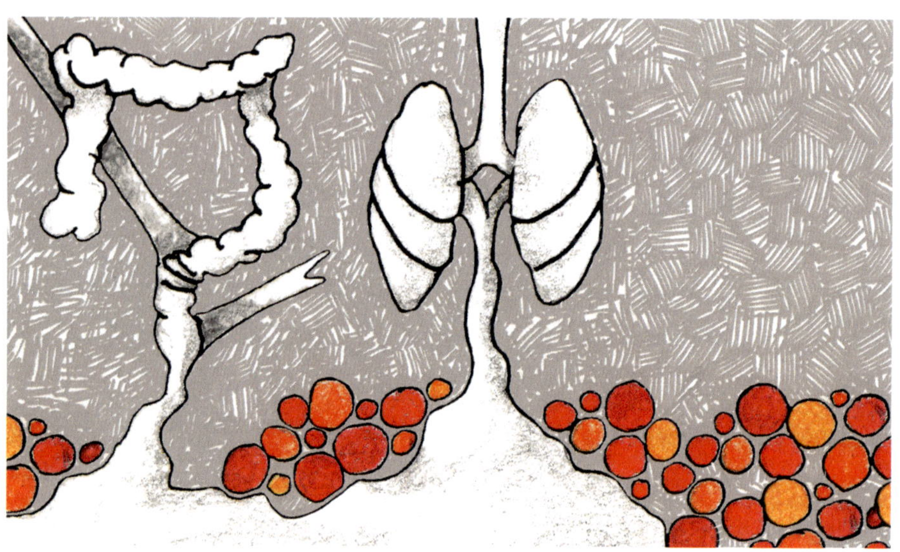

The Spirit of Metal invites you to embrace wellness and aging!

Both organs governed by the Spirit of Metal, the lungs and the colon, embody purification and elimination. The lungs take in oxygen, a life-giving energy, and expel carbon dioxide. They are described in classical Chinese medicine as "the receivers of the pure Chi from the Heavens." Meanwhile, the colon absorbs water, nutrients, minerals, and vitamins and eliminates waste. While the Spirit of Metal encourages you to nourish yourself well and cleanse your colon, she also incites you to breathe in and out fluidly and deeply.

- Practise breath-focused meditation, restorative yoga, Yoga Nidra, and/or other similar disciplines.
- Practise pranayama or other forms of active breath work to deepen your fluid movement practice.
- Learn to breathe efficiently and fluidly when you work out or when you participate in competitive sports.
- Remember to breathe when you work or concentrate.
- Summon your breath to foster mindful presence when interacting with others, especially if you are challenged.

The Spirit of Metal also teaches you not only to accept changes in your body but also to embrace them. While you exercise to activate well-being and health, you are mindful of your changing needs, age, or circumstances and accept aging as the manifestation of Nature's ancient and enduring cycle. Although you cultivate personal fitness and well-being, the Spirit of Metal encourages you not to capitulate to the use of products, therapies, injections, or surgeries exploiting your or others' fear of aging, death, and dying. Furthermore, she beseeches you not to participate in the expansion of this multi-billion-dollar industry that perpetuates a cult of fear, worthlessness, and confusion about aging and dying.

The Spirit of Metal encourages you to consciously connect to your breath to cultivate a generous participation in Nature's regenerative cycle of expansion and contraction, harvest and distribution, embracing and letting go.

LUNGS – COLON – NOSE

SPIRIT OF METAL

Physical Disharmony

39

You may resist imbibing and have a hard time letting go!

Whoops! You live, therefore you breathe; and you breathe, therefore you live—yet you are scarcely alive or vibrant! The Spirit of Metal compassionately witnesses that your sense of self and your place in the world may be obstructed and/or too rigid! Either way, you are contracted and closed off rather than receptive and fluid.

- You may feel stuck or unyielding.
- You may be fixed in a rigid stance that is both resistant and pushes opportunities away.
- You may refuse to "give in" and find yourself trapped in a fighting stance.
- You may hang on to a narrative of what should be rather than take in the beauty and wisdom of what is.
- You see the dark side in everything and focus on all the things that have gone wrong or could go wrong.
- You may swallow your feelings and choke down your grief and shame with food, alcohol, tobacco, and/or illegal/legal drugs.

Consequently, low-vibration emotions are building up and you are unwilling or unable to engage in a fluid exchange with people and all living beings, including the earth and your earth body. The Spirit of Metal beckons you to take heed. You may be trapped in a vicious cycle: disturbances in your lungs and colon may have adverse effects upon your emotional, mental, and spiritual harmony; and your emotional, mental, or spiritual disharmony may impair your lung and colon functions.

The Spirit of Metal encourages you to trust Nature's cycle of expansion and contraction. First, acknowledge your sacred relevance and breathe into it. Second, embrace life's generous yet impermanent offerings and express gratitude. Third, recognize your capacity for service and share your harvest.

DISHARMONY STORY

Your bowels have been off for as long as you can remember, despite the fact that you pay attention to what you eat. You're hopeless at this point because almost everything you eat triggers a tumultuous exodus. You're trying hard and taking lots of supplements, yet it's damage control at best. It's pretty clear you do not absorb the nutrients of the healthy food you prepare because you're chronically underweight and have had pneumonia almost twice a year for the past five years. In addition, it's really debilitating because it seems to be getting worse every year and you can barely keep up with your young child or deal with your erratic partner.

The good news is that the client is married and finally has a baby. A stable-enough relationship was a long time coming, and this is supposed to be their dream come true. Yet their partner's failure to meet their co-parenting expectations bowls them over again and again. Usually by evening they are so worn out and shocked that they spiral into an ever-widening gulf of grief. Besides, each day seems worse than the previous. The child is not the only one who is neglected—they're bursting with loneliness too. While their partner's lack of commitment continues to disappoint them, their partner's increasing volatility whenever they bring up the topic is even more distressing. Their outbursts, which initially seemed incongruous, are now the norm. Although disheartening at first, the escalating aggression gradually erodes the client's perfect nuclear-family dream enough for them to give up on their partner and ask for a divorce.

Yet, a few years down the road, the cries are familiar: "It's outrageous-preposterous-contemptable even! My child must have another parent, even if it is part-time. My child needs this and deserves this. Besides, I waited long enough. If I wanted to do this alone, I would have done it long before!" Predictably, the catalogue of disappointing financial and emotional fiascos is still endless, including the bowel irregularities and back-to-back pneumonias. Although the client is now divorced, they are still trapped in the all-consuming grief and self-pity that incapacitated them during their marriage. "My ex has to change!" they insist.

Unfortunately, the client still envisions a harmonious future that depends on this person's healing, transformation, and evolution. Yet the ball is in their court. It's up to them to grow past this relationship, let go of their attachment to the nuclear-family dream as they imagined it with this person, accept their endless shortcomings even post-divorce, and embrace the abundance of their child's love and everything that comes with the discovery of who that child is. It's up to them to change and grow out of these expectations and liberate themself from the chokingly sad scarcity at the core of this relationship.

39

The Spirit of Metal assists you in identifying what is precious and necessary and teaches you to eliminate anything stale, unnecessary, or harmful. She especially prods you to let go of what is detrimental.

She encourages you to release your leaves so that they may decompose and enrich the soil, thereby nourishing and strengthening Nature's regenerative cycle. She prompts you to make room for new people and experiences to help you learn, grow, and evolve.

LUNGS – COLON – NOSE

SPIRIT OF METAL

Emotional Harmony

40

The Spirit of Metal teaches you to greet grief and soften into its inevitability!

The Spirit of Metal inspires you to live alongside impermanence peaceably. She not only persuades you to meet life's cyclical progression head on but also coaxes you to flow with the cyclical nature of expansion and contraction. She encourages you to create time and space to actively grieve a sudden loss or a predictable loss, such as:

- the end of a relationship;
- the loss of a home, country, culture, job, school, temple, and/or refuge;
- the loss of health, physical ability, and/or independence;
- the loss of a skill or proficiency; and/or
- the loss of financial security.

Whatever it is, the Spirit of Metal assures you of her steadfast support—she is always with you, especially when you soften into the emotions that severance, endings, and conclusions awaken. Thus, the Spirit of Metal incites you to accept endings as an indispensable part of learning, growing, and renewal. Allow her presence to fortify your courage to feel and let your tears flow.

The Spirit of Metal also teaches you to accept the cycle of expansion and contraction communally and globally. While your harvest is inherently enriching and nourishing, it must also be shared with others. Autumn, after all, instigates the loss of your leaves to the earth and incites you to behold the inevitability of rebirth within their decomposition. Hence, Nature's regenerative cycle buttresses your sense of justice and integrity and bolsters your global consciousness, social engagement, and generosity.

The Spirit of Metal inspires you to not only contend with change and transformation but also expect it and invite it. She inspires you to trust the life-sustaining rhythm of change and release, at harvest time and in times of upheaval or transition.

LUNGS – COLON – NOSE

SPIRIT OF METAL
Explosive Emotional Disharmony
41

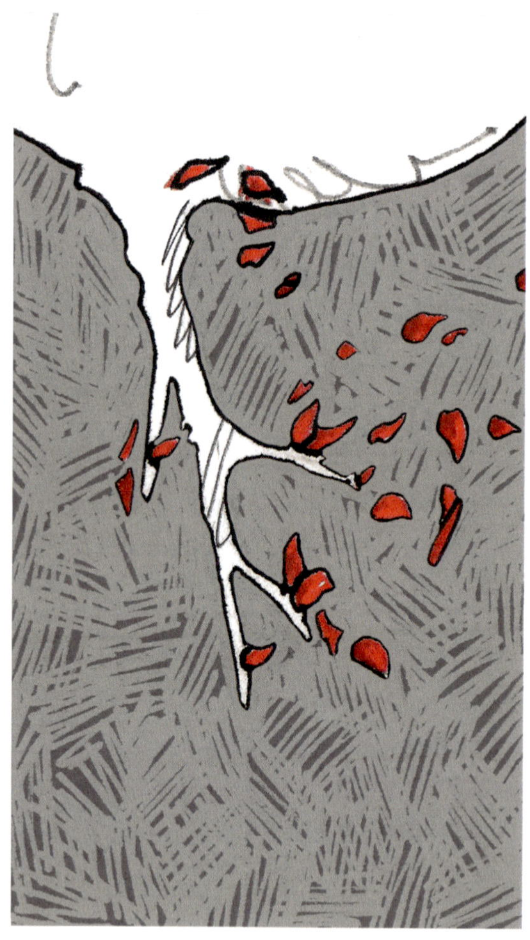

You may have lost your moorings!

Whoa, super heavy. Please know that the Spirit of Metal is right here with you, whether you can feel her compassionate and soothing presence or not. Even though you may feel like the rug has been pulled out from under you and you have lost the plot, know that the Spirit of Metal implores you to lean on her to get your bearings. Her command of the regenerative cycle of expansion and inevitable contraction is colossal. Note to self: You're not alone in this morass of misgivings. This life-affirming rhythm is one of the most misunderstood and doubted in modernity.

On the one hand, you may be overwhelmed by what seems like merciless and relentless contraction and therefore feel grief-stricken, morose, and/or inconsolable. On the other hand, you may evade grief and grieving.

- You may feel weary, exhausted, and/or sleepy a lot.
- You may feel apathetic, numb, and/or shut down.
- You may circumvent opportunities to feel your grief.
- You may isolate yourself to protect yourself from potential disappointment, loss, or grief.
- You may steer clear from people grieving, public displays of grief, and/or situations with built-in opportunities for communal grieving.
- You may rarely cry.

Despite the intensity of autumn's contraction, the Spirit of Metal buoys you. She assures you that the cycle of expansion and contraction is Nature's gift of renewal and rebirth. When trusted and welcomed, the Spirit of Metal's rhythm bolsters your potential to grow and evolve.

DISHARMONY STORY

It's been a hell of a two-year marathon. You nursed your sister, who eventually died of cancer, and you were diagnosed with it too but you are now in remission. Meanwhile, your spouse was AWOL with their own train wreck so you were left to your own devices to support your sister, deal with your own treatments, and keep your shared household afloat. The logistics alone are endless, never mind the howling grief threatening to swallow you whole.

Anyway, it's just so fucking wrong! Your father died when you were in your mid-twenties, your sister did not make it to fifty, your spouse has been super sick for months, and you weren't sure if you would make it to fifty either. Besides, it's not just you: the whole world is going to hell in handbasket. Every day there's a crazy huge environmental, social, geopolitical, or medical tragedy killing innocent people violently or disgracefully! Everywhere you look, untimely death creates immense suffering! What's the point?

Taking a rigid stance vis-à-vis the mystery of life and death is like living life on the edge of a freshly sharpened blade. My favourite line in my all-time favourite allegorical opera, *The Emperor of Atlantis* by Viktor Ullmann, is spoken by the Death character, who finds himself trapped in the midst of a genocide waged by a tyrannical dictator: "I am not a murderer, I am a gardener!" Death exclaims emphatically. Ullmann, the librarian of the Goetheanum and Anthroposophical Society, wrote these words while incarcerated in a Nazi concentration camp. While the implications are obvious within the Second World War context, a greater philosophical wisdom emerges as well. The merciful cycle of life and death includes rebirth. Hence, death is a transformational agent and a caring gardener, even if human beings and nature seemingly foil its warranted grace and dignity often.

The client is not alone in this morass of misgivings. The merciful and life-affirming rhythm of loss, separation, and death are some of the most misunderstood, doubted, and feared in modernity. Most of the clients resist change, refuse to "give in," and assume a fighting stance to beat cancer or keep a relationship or a job, even when it's clear that the relationship or investment is stale, unnecessary, or harmful. Yet cancer is a most prescient messenger. This illness, more than any other I encounter, is a clear voice from the clients' Sacred Trees, exposing an unconscious or willfully buried disorientation. While this client can't control the timing of anything, including death, they can soften enough to discover the profound teachings imbedded in their journey with cancer and their loved ones' physical decline and deaths.

41

In Chinese medicine, grief is one of the most prevalent emotions of the Metal element. Grief cleanses you of what is no longer needed in your life. When the Spirit of Metal is blocked or imbalanced within you, your expression of grief likewise becomes imbalanced and inappropriate. It may be excessive and ongoing. Or, in the other extreme, it may be avoided or suppressed.

The Spirit of Metal encourages you to recognize the might of the expansion and unavoidable contraction impulse of Nature's regenerative cycle. She inspires you to live alongside impermanence peaceably. She persuades you to meet life's cyclical progression head on and incites you to accept endings as an indispensable part of learning, growing, and renewal. Allow her presence to fortify your courage to feel and let your tears flow.

LUNGS – COLON – NOSE

SPIRIT OF METAL

Implosive Emotional Disharmony

42

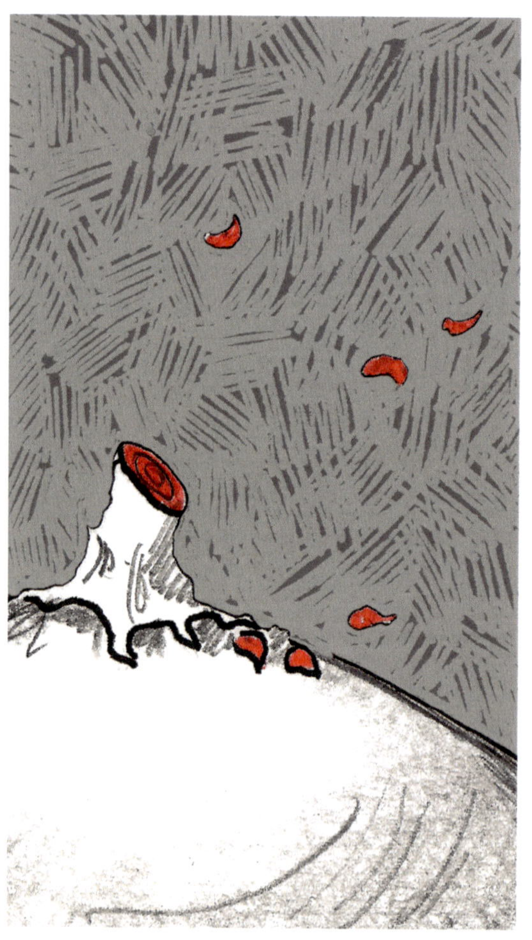

Your dignity may be choked by shame!

Ay, caramba! There's nothing like stealthy shame to knock back your self-worth and service in one fell swoop. The Spirit of Metal recognizes that shame may be suffocating your self-image, self-respect, personal authority, personal power, and, most importantly, your sacred relevance and service simultaneously. In other words, shame not only hushes you inside, it also chokes your output, fairness, generosity, and accountability—you lose big and so do all other living beings.

The Spirit of Metal acknowledges that shame is a powerful agent in the cycle of violence. It silences your most precious resources: the cognizance, recognition, and respect of your sacred relevance and service. Thus, as you are robbed of your internal treasure and capacity to produce a bountiful harvest, this pernicious opponent starves your integrity and dignity, thereby triggering a feeding frenzy often manifesting as a need to take, control, denigrate, or exploit.

- You may feel worthless, inferior, denigrated, mortified, and/or flawed or you impose this on others.
- You may feel scorned, slandered, and/or stigmatized or you impose this on others.
- You may feel guilty, unpardonable, reprehensible, and/or ruined or you impose this on others.
- You may feel contrite, apologetic, and/or repentant or you impose this on others.

Even though you may be ashamed that you were shamed—humiliated that you were humiliated—the Spirit of Metal lends you enough courage to face this mighty adversary and trauma to transcend this cycle's insidious contraction and violence.

DISHARMONY STORY

Your father was on you all the time: "You're a slob! Clean your room!" "Are you stupid or what? Get your shit together at school and do your homework!" "You're a spoiled brat! Help your mom around the house!" It's an endless litany. Your mom was not far behind either. Your days were punctuated by their persistent criticisms. And it's been like this for as long as you can remember, and it still is! You're in your mid-twenties and you still can't get your shit together and your parents are the first ones to call you out on it. Even though you are clean sometimes, you still succumb to using ethyl alcohol and marijuana. You're off the pills, but still, it's a major struggle. So from where you sit most days, it's pretty clear that you're a loser—that's it, that's all.

Regrettably, this is only the tip of the iceberg. We discover in sessions that the invectives laid on the client also included words such as *slut* and *whore*. The client often tumbles into an overwhelming felt-sense of being ugly, disgusting, and gross. When we probe further, we discover that this "loser" child was molested by a family friend when they were three years old. Both their father and mother just thought the child was crazy when they banged their head against the floor; or was really pigheaded when they cried and screamed through the night; or was disgusting when they reached out to adults and children in a seemingly sexual way before the age of five; or was stupid because they weren't even passing grade one. The client's parents failed to witness their child's distress or search compassionately for the root cause. Unfortunately, they persistently interpreted their child's "troublesome" behaviour as the child's failure to measure up and patently ignored their own abusive actions and accountability.

Much later when things really fall apart at school and the shit hits the fan daily, both parents also "forget" the night that the mother pulled their "fucking floozy" teenager out from under a boy in a tent in the backyard and threw them in their room until morning. Likewise, the parents ignore the part about calling the client a drunken slut in front of their brother the next morning. To boot, later that week, the client was assailed by similar slurs by schoolmates all over Facebook. Their mother again neglected to compassionately witness the client even though they told their mother they were shunned and ostracized at school.

Unfortunately, when we probe further into this in sessions, we unveil the truth: they were actually drugged and raped on their birthday in that tent in their backyard on that infamous night. They were then thrown into a room and left alone to ride the very scary and epic experience of being drugged without knowing it, of being raped without knowing it, yet knowing all too well they were disgusting and rightfully discarded. Again, the client's "inherent deficiency" and "failure to measure up" is blamed while the parents fail to acknowledge their blindness and their part in amplifying the trauma.

Brené Brown cleverly refers to shame as a "full-contact" emotion. You are *in shame* rather than suffering a shame wound somewhere, here or there. It's an invasive feeling, more like a noxious weed, that surreptitiously smothers your gardens before you even know it's there. While trapped in its gaze, you lose sight of your strengths, beauty, and sacredness. And "Until we start addressing the role shame plays, we may temporarily fix some of the surface problems, but we can't silence the old tape in our head that suddenly blares some version of 'something is wrong with me.'" (Brené Brown, *I Thought It Was Just Me (but it isn't): Making the Journey From "What Will People Think? to "I Am Enough"*)

Ultimately, shame is the most stealthy and pernicious foe you will ever meet. Although it seems only to lurk in mysterious dark corners, you lug it around everywhere you go and in whatever you do. While it tends to permeate your personal and public lives, it sure as hell doesn't rent a billboard on the highway so that you can really see it either. Rather, it's a silent assailant who peers at you 24/7. It looks at you rather than you at it. In fact, in my practice, I spend more time unearthing these lumbering giants than all other painful experiences combined. I would estimate that 90 percent of the clients are shocked to hear that the distress they are lugging in and experiencing on the table is shame.

When autumn's brisk cool winds wither your leaves and scatter them, the Spirit of Metal grants you a vision of your magnificent essence. She reinforces your self-worth and dignity and assures you that your innate genius and sacred relevance are a wellspring of medicine and life-affirming nutrients.

It's harvest time, after all!
The Spirit of Metal entices you to recognize and savour your Sacred Tree's delicious fruit.

LUNGS – COLON – NOSE

SPIRIT OF METAL

Mental Harmony

43

The Spirit of Metal inspires you to big-heartedly respect your sacred relevance!

The Spirit of Metal is devoted to the manifestation and dissemination of your sacred relevance and service. She emboldens you to recognize and respect your genius as a powerful means to express your wholesome and sacred purpose. She also lends you the courage you need to capitalize on your genius and strengths for the betterment of the world. It's inescapable—each living being carries a much-needed medicine into the earthly realm and implicitly has the duty to share it with all living beings.

Everyone is touched by the magnitude of this vision and the integrity and generosity of the Spirit of Metal's teachings. She decisively bolsters your commitment to conscientiously engage with the world and be part of the solution. She inspires you to consistently enrich yourself and others simultaneously. She emboldens your mindful objectives and your means of production and distribution. And believe you me, she shores you up every step of the way.

- You do not let profits, revenue, and bonuses influence or distort your genius, purpose, objectives, and service.
- You enhance execution, process, and wholesome outcome rather than increase productivity for profit's sake.
- You develop and sustain mindful and responsible means of distribution.
- You create, support, and promote ethical and fair-trade economies.

The Spirit of Metal is committed to you, and in turn she motivates you to produce steadily, competently, and distribute justly.

LUNGS – COLON – NOSE

SPIRIT OF METAL
Explosive Mental Disharmony
44

You may define your self-worth with material gain!

Like, whoa! Where're you going with that? The Spirit of Metal ascertains that you may be prioritizing accumulation over meaning and therefore are focusing on personal gain rather than fair-minded contribution, exchange, and/or distribution.

- You may be running like a chicken with your head cut off to make more and more money.
- You may work long hours to create or maintain a specific job, house, and/or family lifestyle deemed "essential."
- You may be covetous and pine for more money, a better job, a bigger house, a better car, a cottage, and a flashier something and everything.
- You may be motivated by greater and greater grandiosity and pretentiousness.
- You may get high on acquisition, profits, pre-eminence, dominance, and/or control.

The Spirit of Metal acknowledges that it's complex. Often, it's not just about bigger and better for better's sake. You may be on a fiscal achievement bender and/or lurch from trophy to trophy to prop up your self-worth, bearing, and significance. You may also compulsively accumulate possessions, secure money, gain lifestyle attributes, and/or shop to numb your grief and/or shame. In other words, your resolve to compensate may distort your goals, values, and ethics. It's huge!

The Spirit of Metal beseeches you to recognize your genius and learn how to capitalize on your sacred relevance for your evolution and the betterment of the world. She not only animates your resolve but also lends you the courage that you need to manifest your sacred relevance.

DISHARMONY STORY

You are on a one-pointed mission to live the high life with all of its prerequisites: a gorgeous home with a designer decor, a sculpted body with a designer wardrobe, and a favourable marriage with a perfect child. You are intelligent, clever, organized, creative, and super motivated so you soon find a niche in the corporate culture, steadily build up your position, and increase your purchasing power. It's a plus-plus recipe: the more you gain affluence, the more you buy; and the more you buy, the more you achieve control over your environment and your body.

It all looks good and that's the point, but to what end? It never seems to be enough. The client works long hours to make more and more money to afford the latest designer fashions, to enlarge their designer house project, and to escalate their family's lifestyle. It's always deemed essential, and what is essential is ever-increasing. They perennially pine for a better job, a bigger house, a better car, a new look, more shoes, another designer bag, and a flashier something and everything.

It's nothing short of HUGE! While the client sits on top of a mountain of designer possessions, its benefits are no longer vibrant enough to quench their urgent need not only for control but also for burying their truth and shame. Sessions reveal that the client has repressed memories of sexual abuse. The implications run deep, and the collateral damage and pain reach far and wide. By age thirty-five, the client's stockpile of aesthetically pleasing property is useless. It's only the thrill of accumulating that has a charge strong enough to subdue the tumult of their unhealed wounds. Slowly but surely their impulse slips beyond their control, and more and more they reach for their computer, sometimes clicking away thousands in an hour. It's relentless: the thrill of acquiring a new object is only bright enough to blind them for another hour or a day at best, while the shame of addiction prowls around every corner feeding the very beast they wish to bury.

Their mounting need for greater and greater numbing power is frittering away the bedrock of their lives—they are losing personal authority, dignity, and integrity rather than gaining them. Sadly, their resolve to compensate rather than heal trauma has distorted their goals and values, and the disconnection from their Sacred Tree ecology veils the powerfulness of a wholesome in-and-out flow. First, when you heal trauma, you let go of your leaves and they enrich the soil as they decompose. Hence, you participate in Nature's regenerative cycle by surrendering to the wisdom of its built-in contraction and expansion impulses. Second, you create the ideal conditions to reveal your essence and innate genius, which invariably reinforces your sense of self-worth and dignity.

44

The Spirit of Metal fortifies
your capacity to respect
your Sacred Tree ecology.

LUNGS – COLON – NOSE

SPIRIT OF METAL

Implosive Mental Disharmony

45

Your limiting beliefs may smother your aspirations and genius!

Oh boy! Your genius may be cut off from the air it needs to live and thrive. The Spirit of Metal compassionately witnesses that you may be confined by oppressive and inhibiting mandates and beliefs. In fact, you may as well be living with the world's most efficient and cruel sentinel and censor. The Spirit of Metal recognizes that your sacred relevance may be so thwarted that it is virtually obscured. She acknowledges that you might have lost track of your innate medicine quite early on, so much so that you might have stopped evolving in its vigorous light.

- You believe that a livelihood within the corporate sector is the only respectable pursuit and succumb to pressure to settle for a "proper job."
- You believe that predetermined paycheques and annual incomes are the only "sane" or safe life path.
- You believe that you must stay in an unfulfilling job or business to get a steady or big paycheque.
- You believe that you must compete and dominate financially in order to have personal power and authority.
- You believe that you must gain patriarchal accolades and/or hierarchical distinctions to deserve respect, recognition, and love.
- You believe that you must tolerate excessive or abusive corporate expectations to receive a paycheque and/or accolades.

Although your beliefs may temporarily obscure your beauty and meaning, the Spirit of Metal assures you that you carry a much-needed balm to the earthly realm and you implicitly have the duty and pleasure to live in its light and share it with all living beings.

DISHARMONY STORY

You grow up in a tumultuous family in a small town in the middle of the Canadian prairies. The property borders on farmland, and it all seems like a wholesome enough set-up, yet both your parents are tormented by unresolved trauma and are increasingly unstable. By the time you're nine years old, you're fully aware that you need to fend for yourself and generate as level-headed a routine as you can muster. Because if there's one thing you do have, it's a head on your shoulders. You ace it in school and as long as your head is in your homework, you are in touch with a reality where common sense, logic, and orderliness prevail. In fact, you love anything to do with school because you get to cozy up to systems, classifications, and methods. You're desperate for structure and anything that proves that stability and sanity are attainable.

Meanwhile, the upheaval of intergenerational trauma continues to rip though both sides of the family, including you. Unfortunately, the secreted torment of sexual abuse, military involvement, and indoctrination lives on in your parents' shattered lives and disgracefully discharges into yours. While it's hardly a secret that your parents can scarcely get through the day or support a household and a child, the sprawling and devastating impact of intergenerational trauma remains silenced until much, much later. In your mid-teens, you navigate the choppy seas with whatever resources you have: you focus on the attainment of a university degree guaranteed to yield a career deemed respectable (you have to attain self-respect and self-worth somehow) and a high income (you have to support yourself and survive more gracefully somehow).

Unfortunately, the client's perception of the world is painted with one brush: intergenerational trauma. Danger lurks at every corner; shame and disgrace are intrinsic; insanity lies in wait; and paucity is an expected outcome. In other words, if they do not focus on climbing, they may slide into a voracious pit of destitution and this must be avoided at all costs. Therefore, a predetermined sizable annual income is the only sane and safe life path; they must gain patriarchal accolades and hierarchical distinctions to deserve respect, recognition, and love; and they must compete and dominate financially in order to have personal power and authority. The stage is perfectly set: while they are running for their life, they are also running for a career that will eventually choke their life.

Triple OUCH! Regrettably, they lost track of their innate medicine quite early on, so much so that they stopped evolving in its vital light, even as a child and teenager. By their early twenties, the wealth and abundance within them was obscured not only by trauma but also by these firmly planted, inhibiting beliefs. Even though the logic of their survival does not pan out past forty, they soldier on despite increasing depletion, dissatisfaction, and pessimism. The effect is disastrous: the client is cut off from the genius and medicine they need to live and thrive. They are running full speed ahead toward scarcity rather than away from it. Thankfully, after many initiatory experiences (including a scary car accident), the client knows that their life now depends on them initiating a radical 180-degree turn to discover and honour their true genius. The client decisively bolsters their commitment to conscientiously engage with the world and be part of the solution. They finally step away from their firm and embolden their mindful objectives, discovering new means of production and distribution. They now consistently and reliably enrich themselves and others simultaneously. Their pessimism is flattened by their growing amazement and blossoming respect for the power of their genius to make the world a genuinely abundant place for everyone, including them!

The Spirit of Metal emboldens you to recognize your genius as a powerful means to express your wholesome purpose and lends you the courage you need to capitalize on it for the betterment of the world.

It's beautifully built-in: each living being carries a much needed medicine into the earthly realm and implicitly has the duty to savour their harvest and share it with all living beings.

LUNGS – COLON – NOSE

SPIRIT OF METAL

Spiritual Harmony

46

The Spirit of Metal entwines you with the great Earth Mother's enterprise!

46

The Spirit of Metal inspires you to be an open-hearted and open-handed channel for the earth's abundance. First, the dignity she instills in you fosters a noble expression of your genius—your thoughtful work is consistently healing and wholesome. Second, the deep-rooted sense of justice and social responsibility she reinforces expedites the flow of your innate genius into the world—your integrity carries you through to the mindful and conscious proliferation and distribution of your bounty.

Therefore, you magnanimously share your harvest with your families, local communities, and the global community, including the earth. You also consciously and dependably engage with the Earth Mother's abundance, protect her resources, and share her wealth. You deliberately and consistently embrace a nondiscriminatory, fair-minded, and innovative economy and dissemination platform. Furthermore, with the Spirit of Metal in tow, you are astute enough to recognize when you violate yourself, other living beings, or the earth. You're on it!

The Spirit of Metal amplifies your capacity to transcend the limitations of prevailing and imperious commerce with creativity, insight, and grace.

LUNGS – COLON – NOSE

SPIRIT OF METAL

Explosive Spiritual Disharmony

47

Your desire to dominate and generate profit may be out of control!

Yowza! You may be hypnotized by the overriding materialistic culture and thirst for opulent wealth. The Spirit of Metal compassionately witnesses that you may be falling headlong into the dominant culture's trap of self-absorbed, self-interested, and egocentric commotion, preoccupations, and goals. She recognizes that selfishness and triumph may fuel your dedication, competition may energize your resolve and perseverance, and rivalry and hostility may invigorate your commitment.

The Spirit of Metal forewarns that although you may be self-absorbed, you may also unwittingly participate and fortify an unjust and destructive social, cultural, corporate, and/or geopolitical regime.

- You may push so hard to win, preserve, or increase your accumulation, surplus, social institutions, or hegemony that it is to the detriment of your familial, national, and global communities.
- Your feverish hunger for wealth, power-over, influence, and/or supremacy may invigorate an exploitative corporation and/or hegemony of power-over, domination, and colonization.
- You may be an exploitative entrepreneur, CEO, employer, manager, or employee who systemically undermines the personal power and well-being of other employees and/or pillages Mother Earth.

The Spirit of Metal compassionately calls you back to your infinitely renewable resource: your sacred relevance with its built-in dignity, integrity, and generosity.

DISHARMONY STORY

You're way better than you used to be because, truth be told, you sure had a crazy ride to the top a few years back. You grew up in a country ravaged by a decade-long civil war. Your father and brothers fought tooth and nail to hold on to the family home, and they scraped through the indignities of war and prejudice by the skin of their teeth. And so did you, but you had a knack with computers and sought every opportunity to get access. You hungrily searched the screen for a lifeline out of the violent cesspool of discriminatory oppression and injustice you grew up in. The Internet proved to be your vessel into international waters, where all states have the freedom to fish. And fish you did.

You jumped with both feet into the dot-com foray without missing a beat. By the mid-1990s and your early twenties, you were riding the tech surge right out of your devastated country and into luxury hotels. You literally floated on the speculative investment bubble to the top of the world, enjoying all the perks along the way: the sex, drugs, designer clothes, and all-night parties. However, no matter how high you were, literally and figuratively, you sent money home to your family and you kept your head on your shoulders enough to run for it just before the bubble burst. You managed to hold on to your millions and invested in an import/export company. Basically, you "made it" and now you're settling down, meaning you have frequent layovers in a deluxe condo you call home in a peaceful "world-class" city.

At forty-two years old, the client has everything, yet they have nothing. They sit on their designer couch for hours blindly staring at their immense flat-screen TV. While the threat of poverty fed their resolve, competition energized their perseverance, and rivalry invigorated their commitment for two decades, they now sit listless without a drop of fight left in them. No matter how sharp the designer clothing still is, no matter how exquisitely chosen every object is, no matter how astute their art collection is, the client gets nothing out of it anymore. It's not only the dot-com bubble that has burst, it's the hypnotic pull of materialistic corporate culture. It's blatantly obvious to them that opulent wealth does not nourish and sustain them or anyone in their wake.

The client is now aware that while they were self-absorbed, they unwittingly participated and fortified an unjust and destructive social, cultural, corporate, and geopolitical system. Rather than focus on fair trade, they've been waging a brutal war on their corporate opponents and ambushing disenfranchised people in developing countries via unconscionable middlemen. Although they are using corporate weaponry, they are living by the same standards as the political regime oppressing their birth country. Thankfully, they are waking up to the subtle economy of the human spirit, and now know viscerally and intimately the fierceness and squalor of spiritual poverty. They are now focusing their creativity and imagination on sustainable economic ecology and engaging in dynamic dialogue and exchange rather than opposition.

47

The Spirit of Metal instills in you a deep-rooted sense of justice and social responsibility and expedites the flow of your noble genius into the world. She leads you through to the mindful and conscious proliferation and distribution of your bounty.

LUNGS – COLON – NOSE

SPIRIT OF METAL
Implosive Spiritual Disharmony
48

You may be trapped in the vault of the economy!

Gosh, your pants are wearing you rather than the other way around. The Spirit of Metal compassionately witnesses that you are consciously or unconsciously ensnared in the fevered and human-made capitalist and colonialist construct. You might think that you are getting ahead, but ultimately your values and goals may be overcome by this disempowering dominant narrative. The Spirit of Metal compassionately witnesses that you may be fastened to a 9-to-5 treadmill of labour despite overwhelming evidence of boredom and spiritual depletion.

- You make decisions solely based on financial gains or overhead.
- You resolutely increase your income and aspire to get rich quick.
- You hoard and safeguard your wealth.
- You are frugal to a fault.

Furthermore, you may take it for granted that draining, abusive, and/or deceitful practices are built-in and unavoidable.

- You may fail to keep the corporate vultures' goals in check and, by association, neglect your communities and planet.
- You partake of wealth gained on the back of disenfranchised individuals, communities, and/or nations.

The Spirit of Metal recognizes your innate worth and dignity and assures you that your genius and sacred relevance are a wellspring of life-affirming nectar for all living beings.

DISHARMONY STORY

You're successful and your house is paid up and so is your new car. Despite living in a large urban centre, you go beyond the financial demands of purchasing and upkeep, you renovate most of the house, landscape both the front and back yards, and upgrade your car every couple years. You're on top of it both at home and at work. In fact, you are not only reliable, but you're a pro at saving the day. Your partner relies on you to keep the costly household afloat, and despite being freelance, you are in high demand and hired consistently to pull the rabbit out of the hat. You've got it made, and your parents are proud of you to boot. They started from scratch when they emigrated to Canada, and here you are: top-notch professional garnering top-notch wages and living The Life!

It's fantastic but only from the outside looking in. When I compassionately witness the client's day-to-day experience, I see that they keep going despite feeling drained, disappointed, and sorrowful. They are so roped in to the prescribed rigmarole of happiness based on financial security and success that they systemically misinterpret their internal rumblings and underestimate their disorientation. Not only are they unconsciously hemmed in by their parents' trauma-informed financial advice and their spouse's lavish lifestyle expectations, but they are also tethered to work that contradicts their sacred relevance.

They indiscriminately accept contracts from companies that promote unconscionable consumerism and sell products made on the backs of people living in poverty in developing countries. Even though it looks like they are moving away from poverty, they are unintentionally participating in the fevered capitalist and colonialist construct—the very thing that hurt their parents as children and young adults. Basically, for as long as they unwittingly partake of wealth gained on the back of disenfranchised individuals to invest in their family's safety and future, they feel more and more hollow.

Doing something well, getting paid handsomely, and planning for your children's education does not necessarily make you relevant, just, and honourable. Regretfully, the client's harvest is contaminated and fails to feed their spirit and that of their spouse and children too. They need to find their bearings from within, even if it means rubbing against their parents' and spouse's bewilderment, disapproval, and discontent. The clearer and more discerning the client becomes, the more wholesome their Sacred Tree ecology becomes. Eventually, they experience the joy of sharing genuine and enduring abundance with their loved ones. Not everyone necessarily comes on board, but the path is set for all those who wish to grow and evolve in their wake, including their children. The client is assuredly opening the path for their children to become accountable and honourable adults in alignment with their own Sacred Trees. This is a legacy worth its weight in spiritual gold.

48

Lean in on the Spirit of Metal and soon enough you will remember your intrinsic capacity and calling to be an open-hearted and open-handed channel for the earth's abundance.

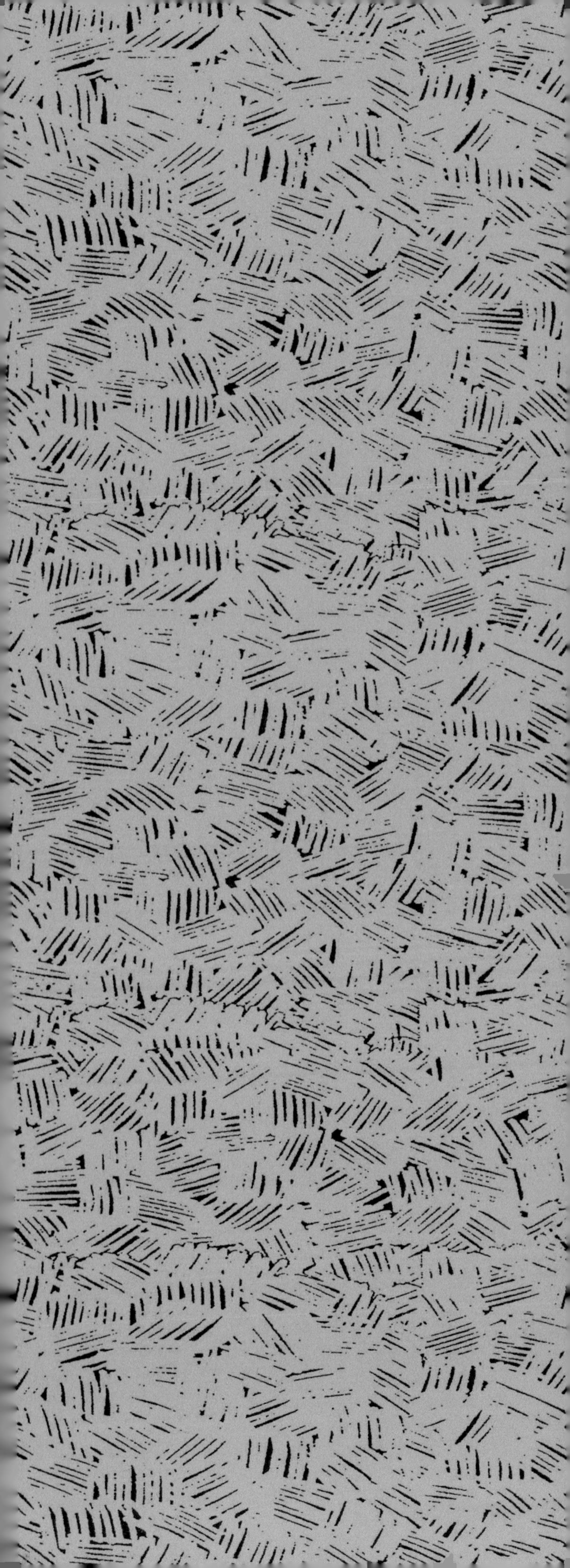

CHAPTER SEVEN

SPIRIT OF WATER

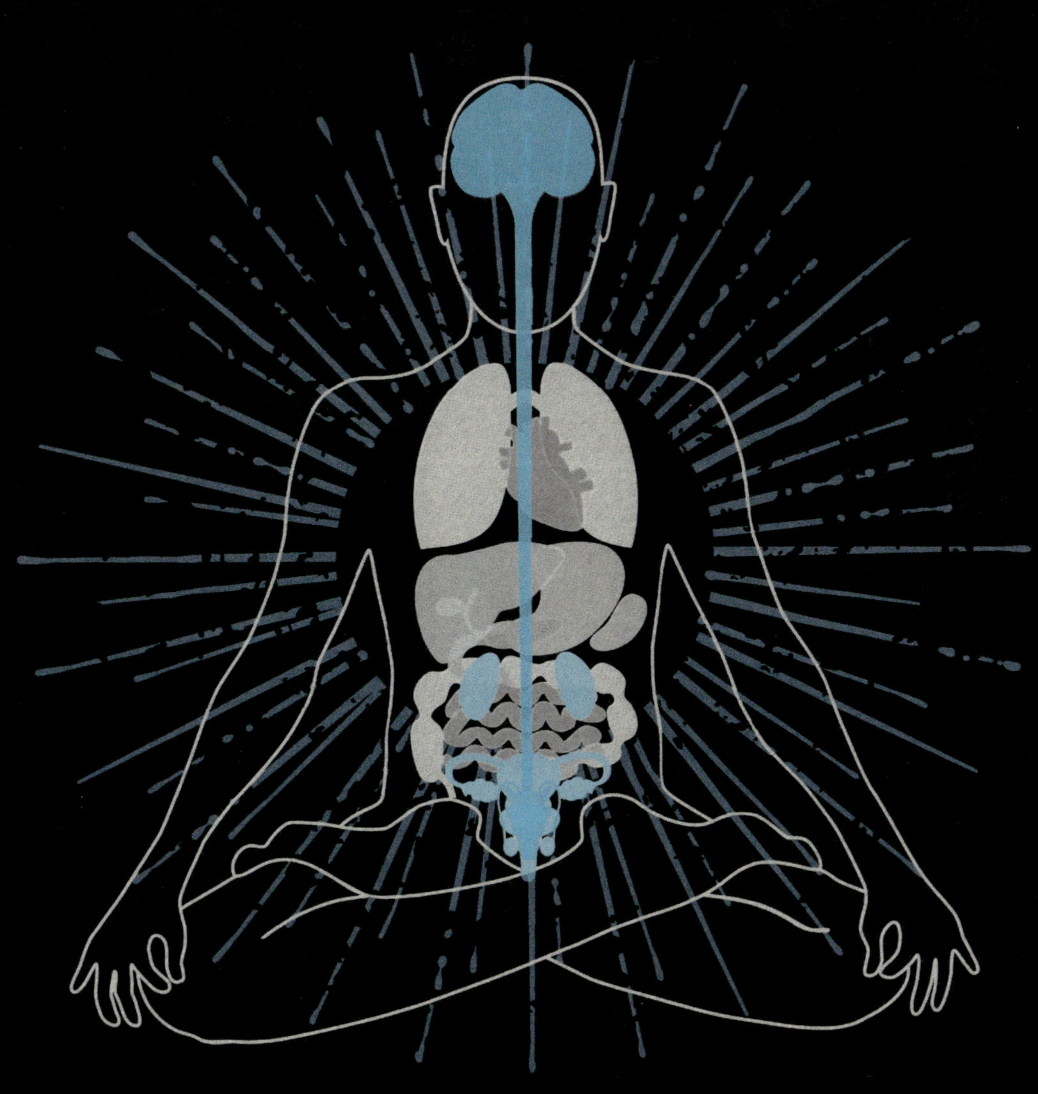

SPIRIT OF WATER

COLOUR	SEASON	YIN ORGANS	YANG ORGANS	EXTERNAL ORGAN
Blue	Winter	Kidneys Reproductive Organs Brain	Bladder Sea of Marrow	Ears

WATER ATTRIBUTES	WINTER PULSE
Seedbed of All Life Reservoir of Willpower and Manifestation Energy Courage and Strength Tidal Rhythms and Cycles Fluidity and Adaptability Path of Least Resistance	Go inside to meet your unadorned essence. Dedicate time to self-inquiry, introspection, reflection, meditation, and concentration. Pay attention to your dreams and visions. Restore energy and reserves. Gather strength for the next cycle of growth.

HARMONY	EXPLOSIVE DISHARMONY	IMPLOSIVE DISHARMONY
HIGH-VIBRATION EMOTIONS	EXPLOSIVE LOW-VIBRATION EMOTIONS	IMPLOSIVE LOW-VIBRATION EMOTIONS
Wisdom Cognizance Willpower Quietude Restfulness Fluidity	Fear Terror Panic Horror Victimization Endangerment	Disorientation Overwhelm Stagnation Aloneness Insecurity Paranoia

EARTH	HARMONY	DISHARMONY	
PHYSICAL	**50** Your earth body merges with Nature's robust rhythms and wisdom. You flow with the seasons. You listen and act on their guidance. Your activities and hormones calibrate accordingly.	**51** You may experience kidney, bladder, brain, reproductive organ, or sea of marrow ailments. Your hormones are out of sync with Nature's cyclical wisdom. Flight–fight–freeze capsizes your wisdom.	
EARTH	**HARMONY**	**EXPLOSIVE DISHARMONY**	**IMPLOSIVE DISHARMONY**
EMOTIONAL	**52** Your stillness and serenity buoy you when you need to step it up and get out from under whatever thumb is oppressing you. You nurture your confidence, courage, and willpower. You live your dreams, NOT your fears.	**53** You may live in an environment saturated with discrimination and abuse. You may be criticized, harassed, controlled, and/or violated in the name of "natural," social, or divine order.	**54** You may be anxious and/or fearful most of the time. You may be easily flustered, overwhelmed, rattled, and/or intimidated. You may often back down from opportunities to grow. You may be browbeaten verbally.
MENTAL	**55** You feed your faith and devotion in stillness and meditation to starve F.E.A.R. (False Evidence Appearing Real). You avoid fearmongering narratives and sensationalist media.	**56** You may believe that others will fall apart if you are not there. You may overwork to feel relevant, respected, or loved despite evidence to the contrary. You may latch on to validation and legitimization.	**57** You may believe that others are more intelligent, capable, or equipped than you are. You may believe that you are weak or broken. You may not be able to hear yourself think past the din of doctrines, propaganda, and/or relentless chatter.
SPIRITUAL	**58** Your evolution mirrors the earth's and the sun's wise cycles. You flow with the potency of your genius and service. You listen to the earth's and the sun's stalwart messengers.	**59** You may be mesmerized by the scarcity meta-narrative. You may be bewildered by the maelstrom of uncertainty and spiritual scarcity in the dominant culture. Your innate wisdom may be capsized by fearmongering.	**60** You may be disoriented. You may persist in relationships and jobs despite dissatisfaction or abuse. You may be absorbed by narratives reinforcing the dominance and relevance of an external world order or security.

KIDNEYS – BLADDER – REPRODUCTIVE ORGANS – BRAIN – SEA OF MARROW – EARS

SPIRIT OF WATER

Sacred Tree in Winter

49

The Spirit of Water invites you to go inside to meet your unadorned essence!

49

The Spirit of Water in winter strips your Sacred Tree right down to its core. Outward signs of life recede: your tree looks skeletal without its external ornamentation and your sap sinks into your roots.

- The Spirit of Water points you to the dark, quiet pool within where your essence resides. She is the elemental Spirit of stillness, tranquility, introspection, and meditation. She encourages you to take the time to cultivate inner fulfillment, peace, and wisdom—she teaches you to be quiet enough to listen and empty enough to be filled.
- The Spirit of Water lures you into the quietness deep within to replenish your energy and gather your strength. She coaxes you into replenishing your spiritual storehouse to stoke your inner courage and willpower—the distilled essence of your manifestation energy.
- The Spirit of Water also cautions you to rest, repair, and regenerate to build up a concentrated, internal vigour strong enough to propel your dynamic growth and cyclical rebirth in the spring.

The Spirit of Water is nothing less than Nature's sturdy metronome. The rise and fall of water levels caused by the gravitational forces exerted by the moon and the sun and the rotation of the earth joins all the elemental Spirits together in a rhythmic dance uniting the earth, the sun, and all living beings. More tangibly than any other elemental Spirit, she reminds you via your hormonal cycles that you are a part of Nature and living by the pulse of her life force. Whatever human-centric plot you may be entangled in, her cadence and cycles live in you, through you, and despite you.

Finally, the Spirit of Water is the element of flow, ease, and adaptability. She motivates you to find the path of least resistance, such as water streaming downhill. She also inspires you to be adaptable, such as water effortlessly responding to its environment by taking the exact shape of whatever contains it, filling every hollow, and yielding to every protrusion.

Slow down, gather your strength, and soften into the flow of wisdom. Invite her sacred tides and cycles to nourish, inform, and orchestrate your rhythm, concentration, and commitment.

KIDNEYS – BLADDER – REPRODUCTIVE ORGANS – BRAIN – SEA OF MARROW – EARS

SPIRIT OF WATER

Physical Harmony

50

The Spirit of Water motivates you to stand on your own two feet!

The Spirit of Water cautions you to follow Nature's invitation to rest, restore, and recharge. She is calling on you to reinforce your commitment to stay on track with your restorative practices and routines, especially if it's winter.

- Your endocrine system, including all hormone-producing glands, needs you to stay relaxed to sync up with Nature's abiding yearly, monthly, daily, and hourly cycles. Your slower pace allows your hormones, the chemical messengers that play a key role in making sure your body is well, to merge with the earth's creating and regenerating impulse.
- Your kidneys, containing the root energy nourishing all your organs and tissues, need you to maintain your measured pace and stay hydrated to support your reserve energy and replenish organs and tissues running low on qi.
- Your brain and the sea of marrow in which it floats also benefit from your gentle and mindful tempo. For instance, you are creating ideal conditions that facilitate the healing of trauma and post-traumatic stress. Hence, you are activating your core consciousness and priming yourself for expansive growth.

The Spirit of Water lures your sap back into your roots. She invites you into the quietness deep within to drink from the wellspring of your innate wisdom, cognizance, willpower, and fluidity—the distilled essence and the source of your manifestation energy.

KIDNEYS – BLADDER – REPRODUCTIVE ORGANS – BRAIN – SEA OF MARROW – EARS

SPIRIT OF WATER

Physical Disharmony

51

You may be out of sync with Nature's rhythm and cycles!

Take heed, as you may be burning the candle at both ends! The Spirit of Water acknowledges that you may be exhausted, depleted, and running yourself ragged. She beseeches you to respect your body's need to rest and restore. She also petitions you to honour winter's wise counsel to go within to the dark, quiet pool where your essence resides. She encourages you to take the time to drink from your innate fountainhead of wisdom, cognizance, willpower, and fluidity.

This regenerative phase of the cycle is the most unappreciated and distorted of all. It is easy to fall prey to the dominant narrative of inevitable, taxing outward production, whether it's social, fiscal, or religious. For instance, cultural traditions such as hectic Christmas holiday expectations and unremitting corporate demands blatantly ignore the needs of human beings during the longest nights of the year.

You may experience ailments in your kidneys, bladder, reproductive organs, endocrine system, or brain. You may also be trapped in a vicious cycle: disturbances in your kidneys, bladder, reproductive organs, brain, or sea of marrow have adverse effects upon the emotional, mental, and spiritual harmony of your water orb; and your emotional, mental, or spiritual disharmony impairs your kidneys, bladder, reproductive organs, brain, or sea of marrow functions.

The Spirit of Water inspires you to listen to your body and trust your innate power to heal and transform. She advises you to slow down enough to acknowledge that your illnesses, dis-eases, and physical manifestations of disharmony are messages your spirit is attempting to transmit: "Something is wrong. You are ignoring something very important. You are not paying attention to your whole self."

The Spirit of Water prompts you to listen, comprehend, and heed your body's messages to uncover and eventually heal the root of the dysfunction, illness, and disharmony rather than turning in circles and managing symptoms.

DISHARMONY STORY

Basically, you work day and night. On the one hand, you are on a roll creatively and developing stimulating relationships with like-minded artists, collaborators, and producers. On the other hand, you work well under pressure and tend to meet your deadlines reliably. Besides, you don't have children so you have a flexible schedule and respond well to the demands of international travel and manifesting stage designs in various urban centres simultaneously. Despite your time and focus being split in a hundred different directions between the various productions, artistic visions, lighting designers, production and technical directors, divas, carpenters, welders, cutters, tailors, sewers, sculptors, painters, organizers, and dis-organizers, you're on it. In fact, you're so in the flow that you conveniently only get your period on opening nights. So, if four operas and a play premiere in a year, you get your period five times. Forget the gravitational pull of the moon and the sun on the oceans—your body of water is on a whole other more vital program.

Needless to say, that whole rigmarole was not sustainable. This is not a client's history; it's the end game of my exciting, rewarding, and unsustainable career in theatre and opera stage design. When early peri-menopause hurtled in at age thirty-eight with its whole host of symptoms—such as hot flashes, fatigue, and irregular periods that turned out to be three-week-long periods with only a two-week break in between—I nearly lost my mind. By the time I stopped bleeding at forty, I was fit to be tied. When I was officially menopausal, two years after the last episode of bleeding like a stuck pig, I crashed right out. I slept for eighteen hours a day for three months, then fourteen hours nightly for eight more months, all the while closing my career as a designer, ending a ten-year relationship, divorcing my parents due to their obstinate denial of the truth, and concluding my epic joyride on adrenaline.

Stress hormones, your "homegrown" drugs of fear, are designed for high performance in moments of crisis. Adrenaline and cortisol are normally secreted in response to a perceived and exceptional threat in the environment by preparing your body to either stay and deal with the threat, run away to safety, or play dead. This fight–flight–freeze response gives organisms an evolutionary advantage by making them better able to survive by increasing their chances of either destroying the threat or escaping it. As such, they are not designed for accelerated daily attainment or simply for waking up in the morning. You could have fooled me—I didn't leave the house before I had at least two expressos on a normal day, never mind when I had pressing deadlines or overnight and overseas travel going into a full of day of work!

With coffee shops on every corner dispensing caffeine and sugar—effective delivery systems for adrenaline and cortisol—these stress hormones have become as essential for waking as opening your eyes. Our culture and market economy create, support, and enable the endemic addiction to your own body's chemistry of fear. It's enough that most of you, me included, have been revved up on stress hormones since childhood due to shock and trauma. Yet we routinely crank up the old fear program, which does nothing to quell the storm of post-traumatic stress and increases our distance from wisdom, cognizance, quietude, restfulness, and wholesome fluidity—the specific high vibrations we need to heal.

The Spirit of Water is nothing less than Nature's sturdy metronome. More tangibly than any other elemental Spirit, she reminds you via your hormonal cycles that you are a part of Nature and living by the pulse of her life force. Whatever human-centric plot you may be entangled in, her cadence and cycles live in you, through you, and despite you.

51

KIDNEYS – BLADDER – REPRODUCTIVE ORGANS – BRAIN – SEA OF MARROW – EARS

SPIRIT OF WATER

Emotional Harmony

52

The Spirit of Water forewarns that fear is your guide, not your master!

52

The Spirit of Water emboldens you to use fear to bring out the best in you. She teaches you that fear is a form of heightened awareness that amplifies your ability to perceive opportunities and adversity clearly. Either way, she buoys you when you need to learn the most from a situation, stand on your own two feet, and, most importantly, stay on track with your sacred relevance. Hence, she teaches you that fear is not an excuse to capitulate, come to a standstill, or a good enough reason to quit. Quite to the contrary, she reminds you that fear is your cue to do something new, big, uncertain, and audacious. It's a call to action to get out from under whatever thumb is oppressing you and threatening the manifestation of your genius.

Nevertheless, the Spirit of Water encourages you to regroup via timely appointments with your innate deep pool of wisdom and willpower in order to consistently use fear as a friend. She prompts you to join her in a bathtub, pool, lake, river, or ocean often enough and long enough to remember the beauty of silence and the guidance it brings. She especially implores you to relish in her watery embrace if you feel disoriented, overwhelmed, alone, or gripped by apprehension, fear, or terror. The Spirit of Water's stillness and serenity is a superlative resource to uplift you when you need to step it up or to keep you afloat despite adversity.

Courage is not the absence of fear but rather the recognition that your inner wisdom, willpower, and genius are more important than fear.

KIDNEYS – BLADDER – REPRODUCTIVE ORGANS – BRAIN – SEA OF MARROW – EARS

SPIRIT OF WATER

Explosive Emotional Disharmony

53

You may live in an environment saturated with discrimination and abuse!

Holy moly, you may be attacked in the name of a "natural," social, or divine order! The Spirit of Water compassionately witnesses that sexist, racist, heterosexist, ethnocentric, xenophobic, colonialist, classist, ageist, or other subtle or overt pecking orders may be sanctioned and implemented by an undisputed "natural," social, or divine order in your home, community, and/or nation. Oppressors, for instance, may uphold their hurtful actions with the offensive claim that "I'm doing this in the name of an incontestable 'natural,' social or divine order." Unfortunately, you, your elders, and your ancestors may be trapped in a vicious cycle of cruelty for generation after generation. Hence, you may consciously or unconsciously suffer and/or participate in its insidious cycle of disrespect and absolutism.

- You may be routinely neglected, criticized, snubbed, ostracized, and/or discriminated against or you do so to others.
- You may be scolded, punished, and/or harassed in the name of a "natural," social, or divine order or you do so to others.
- You may be mocked, belittled, and/or humiliated in the name of a "natural," social, or divine order or you do so to others.
- You may be blamed, slandered, vilified, and/or publicly humiliated in the name of a "natural," social, or divine order or you do so to others.
- You may be colonized, undereducated, overworked, and/or under-rewarded or you do so to others.
- You may be routinely frightened, intimidated, bullied, raped, exploited, tyrannized, and/or enslaved or you do so to others.

The Spirit of Water encourages you to join her in a bathtub, pool, lake, river, or ocean, especially when you feel gripped by fear and confusion. Remember her and summon her! Her stillness and serenity is a superlative resource to uplift you and enlighten you despite treacherous misperceptions, subjugation, and cruelty.

DISHARMONY STORY

You're a staunch serial monogamist despite all the bullshit that comes with most people you date, such as lying, cheating, addiction mayhem and duplicity, verbal abuse, shaming, manipulation, and possessiveness. Often you succumb to flashy relationships with wealthy older people who stealthily demand sexual returns or, at worse, impose non-consensual sexual activity. Regrettably, your ability to dissociate spontaneously serves you well or, rather, serves your partners well. Despite knowing with your head that these sexist jerks are crossing the line, you compulsively fall for their effusive flattery and declarations and "fall in love."

Unfortunately, your implacable fear of being alone obstinately roars more loudly than your ardent feminist awareness and exasperation. On the one hand, you are well aware of the duplicitous celebration and exploitation of your physical beauty since early childhood. It was obvious you were a prey dangling in the watering mouths of wolves when in your teens. You were not only coerced into beauty pageant competitions, an environment ripe with sexual harassment and exploitation, but you also modelled in the equally misogynist fashion industry. Even though you were not aware of the extent of the trauma when steeped in it, you experienced endangerment, victimization, fear, and horror consciously. You never forgot all that crazy shit! On the other hand, it's been far trickier to get a handle on the ubiquitous sexual abuse you experienced at home. Until relatively recently, you had no memories of the sexual violation and exploitation perpetrated and orchestrated by your father.

Initially, as a child, the client was drawn to sweets to numb their feelings and facilitate dissociative amnesia to survive sexual abuse. As a teenager, they added caffeine pills to their compulsive candy consumption, especially when competing or modelling to withstand the long hours and mitigate the inevitable sugar crashes. Expectedly, they also controlled their food intake and suppressed their appetite with diet pills to deliver the championed thin, marketable, and sexually desirable body. Can you imagine? The client was not only systemically neglected, humiliated, colonized, intimidated, exploited, raped, and enslaved for more than fifteen years, but they are also surviving their abuse by amplifying their normal hormonal response to danger with an extreme stress-hormone-inducing cocktail.

They were still a teenager, remember; they were growing and constructing their adult body and hormonal ecology. The hit of fear, whether circumstantial or chemically induced, was and still is their trustworthy knight in shining armour. Basically, they are still too pumped up and "high" on their ecology of fear to join the Spirit of Water in a bathtub, pool, lake, river, or ocean long enough to tap into their abundant Sacred Tree ecology ripe with wisdom and cognizance. Just when they need sound advice the most, they accelerate rather than decelerate. Hence, the beauty of silent solitude and the guidance it brings eludes them. Instead, they fight their way out of an abusive relationship and fly into the arms of the next guy. The thrust of the stress-hormone rhythm trumps their access to their Water's superlative capacity to inform and uplift them specifically when they need to step it up to really get out from under the thumb oppressing them—not that person or that other person but the warped panic button itself. Only the deep pool of wisdom and willpower within their wholesome Sacred Tree ecology can transform fear into a friend and guide rather than their slave master.

The Spirit of Water teaches you that fear is not an excuse to jump into the next relationship before tuning in to your inner landscape. Quite to the contrary, fear is a call to action to get out from under whatever thumb is oppressing you, including fear itself.

53

SPIRIT OF WATER

Implosive Emotional Disharmony

54

You may be fearful most of the time!

Whoa, you may be browbeaten and intimidated! The Spirit of Water compassionately witnesses that you may be subjected to a verbally and emotionally abusive environment organized by an oppressor to control and dominate you.

54

- You may be consistently intimidated and overwhelmed by the force and might of an oppressor's verdicts and rules.
- You may be frightened or terrified by their behaviours and actions.
- You may be hypnotized by their overbearing and imperious mythology.
- You may be unable to identify or sidestep their manipulative tactics.

The Spirit of Water acknowledges the cumulative impact of oppression and verbal abuse. You may be so disoriented and overwhelmed that you do not have access to your innate personal power, wisdom, and willpower to navigate your way past this volatile and stormy sea. Unfortunately, your life-affirming connection to your sacred relevance and your capacity to flow with its medicine is consciously or unconsciously hindered.

- You may be overwhelmed, discombobulated, and/or freeze when you cannot predict or control outcomes.
- You may be unsettled, frightened, and/or terrified when a turn of events capsizes your expectations, traditions, plans, routines, and/or habits.
- You may consistently back down from tasks outside your habitual scope, challenges, and/or tests.
- You may shrink away from situations demanding creative problem-solving and/or opportunities to learn and grow.

The Spirit of Water emboldens you to use fear to bring out the best in you. She encourages you to tap into fear's gift of heightened perception to distinguish adversity from opportunities.

Most importantly, remember that you are not alone! The Spirit of Water buoys you when you most need to learn from a situation and stand on your own two feet to stay connected to your sacred relevance.

DISHARMONY STORY

You're overwhelmed on a good day. On a bad day, you swing from the ceiling fan at high speed, becoming more and more rattled and frightened. And on a really bad day, you're so unsettled that you freeze and lose the plot entirely. For years now, you've had your strategies and perennially manouevre your way back to some plot, even if it is a mindless routine.

First, you tend to duck for cover and hide out at home as often as possible. Overwhelm might as well be your middle name, so you know yourself well: you always feel more secure when you reduce opportunities for challenging encounters. Most of the time, this means getting away from people, especially your family. Often, it also means getting away from yourself too by using a sizable dose of your favourite anaesthetics: Netflix and YouTube. Second, you consistently back down from demanding duties in the workplace. While you can't avoid going to work (you need to earn your living somehow), you back down from opportunities and tasks outside of your comfort zone. You latch on to familiar work, even if it's unsatisfying to avoid escalating demands, tests, trials, or opposition.

In other words, you've had a good thing going for years until the biological clock eroded your self-willed strategy. You now add parenthood to your long list of fear-inducing triggers, but you no longer have the option to freeze, isolate, or check out. The routines and habits you have carefully crafted to predict and control outcomes to avoid becoming discombobulated are completely out the window—there is nothing quite like an infant or child to capsize your household, habits, and plans. You're losing it and your marriage, childcare, and job are in tatters.

While the client is aware of many childhood traumas and has done some healing work, they were surprised to hear that they had an extremely traumatic birth. Their mother did not indicate to them that anything extraordinary or unfortunate had occurred. For one, the client's mother had an epidural, the most commonly used method of pain relief for labour. She was desensitized from the waist down and lost track not just of her pain but also her capacity to sense her baby. In addition, when a crisis occurs during labour, medical personnel often do not inform the mother to avoid a panic reaction. In this case, I sense the staff were on alert due to meconium in the amniotic fluid, decreased fetal movement, and an accelerated heart rate.

54

Cleverly, the client was playing dead. They knew they could not afford one more potentially fatal tumble. More like a kitten tangled in a ball of wool than a baby adequately positioned for birthing, the client has their umbilical cord tightly wrapped around their neck. The threat is real, the shock is in proportion to the danger, and their freeze response is both a reaction and a successful strategy to survive. Their immobility saved their life. Hence, the client's limited market survey of life on the earth is marked by life-threatening danger and their successful possum strategy. While birthing makes an impression on all of us, those of us who experience a life-threatening transition have these conditions imprinted as a baseline: life is scary and whatever worked then is the go-to for that person until unacknowledged and unprocessed trauma is released from their kidneys and adrenal glands. This release is not an immediate miracle solution, but it's a firm step in the process of thawing and unwinding a hindering foundational blueprint.

The Spirit of Water is the element of flow, ease, and adaptability. She encourages you to find the path of least resistance, such as water streaming downhill, and motivates you to be adaptable, such as water effortlessly responding to its environment by taking the exact shape of whatever contains it, filling every hollow, and yielding to every protrusion.

KIDNEYS – BLADDER – REPRODUCTIVE ORGANS – BRAIN – SEA OF MARROW – EARS

SPIRIT OF WATER

Mental Harmony

55

The Spirit of Water inspires you to transcend fear!

The Spirit of Water foretells that fear thwarts your sacred relevance, especially if you allow it to grow louder than your innate wisdom. First, she inspires you to cultivate stillness in a meditative state to starve F.E.A.R. (False Evidence Appearing Real) and help you recognize that it often stems from a belief that things will not work out or that you need to focus on self-protection. Second, she encourages you to face your fear to build your courage and willpower. She asserts that consistent action overcomes fear and breeds confidence while inaction breeds more doubt and fear. Whichever way, she forewarns that fear is a vicious vortex you can easily fall into.

Therefore, the Spirit of Water beseeches you to trust timely introspection to steer your effort and actions away from fear and toward your sacred relevance—it is ultimately the path of least resistance. Hence, when the Spirit of Water whispers wisdom in your ear, acknowledge her insights and take on whatever bold and creative actions in alignment with your genius she brings to light. In the meantime, always be mindful of what you let in consciously or unconsciously. Steer clear of enervating noise as much as possible.

- Avoid fearmongering and sensationalist media.
- Avoid fear-based advice and hegemonies.
- Avoid hanging out with people who are governed by fear.

The more you transcend fear,
the more you get your genius out there
and get on with your service.
Believe and live your dreams, not
your fear.

KIDNEYS – BLADDER – REPRODUCTIVE ORGANS – BRAIN – SEA OF MARROW – EARS

SPIRIT OF WATER

Explosive Mental Disharmony

56

You may be hooked on external validation!

Eek, you may latch on to external substantiation for dear life! On the one hand, the Spirit of Water compassionately witnesses that you may create a vortex of all-consuming indispensability at home or at work to feel needed, loved, and safe.

- You may believe that you are worthy or loved only when you support others' feelings, needs, desires, life purposes, and aspirations.
- You may believe that you are nourished and divinely rewarded when your service centres solely on the well-being and evolution of others.
- You may even work yourself to the bone to provide careless, corrupt, or abusive people with what they need to feel comfortable, healthy, and proficient. Hence, your indispensability makes meaning out of neglect and disrespect.

On the other hand, the Spirit of Water witnesses that you may alarmingly prize external authentication over your sacred relevance to feel adequate, important, and/or superior.

- You may be moulded by external validation, legitimization, authorities, endorsements, and/or sanctioned certifications.
- You may be influenced or swayed by compliments, praise, accolades, and/or tributes.
- You may do whatever you need to do to be noticed, prominent, famous, and/or commemorated.

The Spirit of Water calls you back to the fountainhead of your Sacred Tree: your sacred relevance.
The Spirit of Water foretells that fear thwarts your genius, especially if you allow it to grow louder than your innate magnificence.

DISHARMONY STORY

You prioritize your devotional life. Becoming a good person is the central tenet of your life and has been for as long as you can remember. You study for hours a day and serve in your religious community in whatever way possible. In fact, your commitments are extensive. You unquestionably attend all services and celebrations; you attend as many classes as possible to deepen your understanding of your faith's spine; you are involved at the organizational level and participate in multiple committees; you fundraise; you passionately lead a much-needed women's study group; and your door is always open and teapot always ready to offer much-needed reassurance and comforting.

It's a lot for most, but your fear that it's never enough propels you forward. You don't just attend the service, you arrive early to help set up and leave late to help clean up; you don't just look forward to the lovely annual picnic, you bring loads of homemade treats; you don't just show up for class, you enthusiastically bring well-thought-out questions; you don't just attend the meeting, you bring a spreadsheet to help the group see an issue more clearly and make a better decision; you don't just fundraise to support the organization, you push ahead to create support groups for women; you don't just teach, you prepare for days ahead and stay late to hold space for students who have pressing questions or emotional needs; and often you don't just invite distraught people over for tea, you offer a specialized therapeutic session for free.

I'm exhausted just writing this. Yet what I describe is the tip of the iceberg. This is only the client's devotional schedule; it doesn't include their strenuous familial responsibilities and relentless professional commitments, which overlap with their devotional enthusiasm. The client's heart is open to Divine love, there's no question, and there hasn't been any since childhood. Yet their life has been defined by their ardent and relentless quest to deserve respect, appreciation, approval, safety, and love. Are they good enough to be esteemed and loved by their mother, father, sister, and brother-in-law? Are they good enough to be esteemed and loved by their friend, boyfriend, spouse, colleague, supervisor, and leader? Are they good enough to be esteemed and loved by their schoolteacher, professor, and spiritual mentor?

Consequently, most of the client's relationships are beleaguered by the acquired belief and internalized belief and taskmaster: the fear that they are not enough. Although they urgently create a vortex of indispensability to deserve attention, kindness, consideration, safety, and love, they actually jeopardize their Sacred Tree ecology and relevance by indiscriminately leaking their life force and moulding their relevance into whatever form is deemed worthy enough to receive praise, validation, legitimization, safety, and sanctioned certifications.

56

This ecology is unsustainable at best. At worst, the client works themself to the bone to provide careless, corrupt, or abusive people with what they need to feel comfortable, healthy, and proficient. Tragically, their indispensability can make meaning out of neglect and disrespect. Hence, their conviction and the systemic lack they perceive within unwittingly produces external conditions that sink their Sacred Tree into a cesspool of unlove, the very thing they fear the most.

The Spirit of Water urges you to trust your internal creation matrix and the inherent logic and beauty of your interconnected ecosystem. Your capacity to create and experience love, harmony, and abundance depends on it.

KIDNEYS – BLADDER – REPRODUCTIVE ORGANS – BRAIN – SEA OF MARROW – EARS

SPIRIT OF WATER

Implosive Mental Disharmony

57

You may believe in others more than yourself!

Uh-oh, you may not be able to hear yourself think! The Spirit of Water acknowledges that you may be drowning in a tidal wave of chatter, personal opinions, plodding sermons, propaganda, and/or gossip perturbing your quietude. The relentless flow of oppressive external stimuli may be consciously or unconsciously distorting your capacity to know your sacred relevance, Sacred Tree-ness, and your unique standpoint.

- Oppressive religious dogma, doctrines, and rules may drown out your innate wisdom and personal authority.
- Tenacious and thunderous propaganda may garble your stillness and obscure your inner guidance.
- Someone's commitment and steadfastness to your conversion may feel like love; therefore, you believe that you must listen and disregard your inner guidance.

The Spirit of Water beckons you to slow down long enough to compassionately witness your suffering. Although we often use the term *confusion* lightly, sinking in a morass of disorientation, overwhelm, stagnation, aloneness, insecurity, and/or untruth is extremely wearisome and distressing. Regrettably, your awareness of your innate Sacred Tree may be threatened by the proliferation of the insidious belief systems these conditions often generate.

- You may believe that others are more intelligent, knowledgeable, authorized, and/or capable than you are.
- You may believe that you need others' knowledge, opinions, and/or wisdom to interpret the world for you and/or navigate in the world on your behalf.
- You may believe that you are more vulnerable and thus need protection or others' strength, intelligence, and/or knowhow to dispel potential threats.
- You may believe that you are impaired, spoiled, broken, and/or inadequately prepared to meet the task of living your life.

The Spirit of Water witnesses your powerful Sacred Tree with intact roots, trunk, and branches, no matter what others say or you believe. Although external conditions can give rise to disorientation, the Spirit of Water acknowledges your birthright and innate capacity to connect with your wisdom and willpower to transcend subjugation and ineffectuality.

DISHARMONY STORY

Your caregiver tends to sacrifice for you more times than God can count by 9 a.m. They worry about you 24/7. You are their pride and joy, and they are your best friend. They love to talk on the phone when you're having a disagreement with someone or when you don't know what to do about a situation at work. They always help you unpack your feelings and figure out what you're thinking and help you make decisions about just about everything. Although they seem to know you better than you know yourself, lately you feel uncharacteristically anxious and malcontent. On the one hand, you still believe that you are the person who they tell you you are; but on the other hand, you face swelling aloneness and disorientation.

You are slowly but surely waking up to the reality that what they think is right for you doesn't feel right anymore. You're drowning in their chatter and personal opinions and feel more and more smothered by their values, fears, and unconscious biases. You are propelled forward at full throttle toward greater self-awareness despite the destabilization that you feel when you acknowledge they probably love the person they think you are rather than who you really are. Gradually, you recognize the extent to which you do not know your self and rarely yield to your own curiosity or relax into independent exploration. Eventually, it's plain as day that you haven't navigated the great enterprise of living your own life autonomously.

By the time the client walks in the door, they are acutely conscious that they have lived in a self-interested mirage created by their caregiver and can't hear themselves think. Unfortunately, they were lovingly colonized right out of their Sacred Tree ecology and now feel desperate for meaning and relevance. Like so many others in similar situations with family, partners, or career, they are waking up and smelling the coffee during one of life's built-in initiatory junctures, whether it's one of their Saturn returns (when Saturn cycles back to its position when we were born, at the ages twenty-eight, fifty-six, and eighty-four approximately) or around age forty-two, one of the seminal seven-year-cycle portals often referred to as the midlife crisis.

Thankfully, a bright light is on in the room and they realize that they feel confused about virtually everything. This is the rousing gift built-in to these initiatory portals. While they know what their caregiver or partner or boss thinks they should do, they are now keenly aware that they have no idea what they want to do. They felt so loved and appreciated and yet now they recognize how thwarted, overmanaged, and colonized they are. The relentless flow of oppressive opinions and expectations, previously understood as love, has distorted their capacity to know their Sacred Tree ecology, sacred relevance, and unique standpoint.

57

The Spirit of Water celebrates your innate power to discover, know, and live your dreams!
She beseeches you to trust timely introspection to steer your effort and actions toward your sacred relevance. Hence, when the Spirit of Water whispers wisdom in your ear, acknowledge her insights and take on whatever bold and creative actions she brings to light.

In the meantime, always be mindful of what you let in. Steer clear of external opinions and enervating chatter as much as possible.

KIDNEYS – BLADDER – REPRODUCTIVE ORGANS – BRAIN – SEA OF MARROW – EARS

SPIRIT OF WATER

Spiritual Harmony

58

The Spirit of Water inspires you to unite your innate wisdom and spiritual allies!

The Spirit of Water inspires you to honour Nature's invitation to go within, whether it's winter or not. She is summoning you deep into the roots of your Sacred Tree, encouraging you to eagerly delve into your essence to uncover your inner light and bask in the vigour of your innate wisdom.

- Listen for accessible guidance.
- Follow the trail of insights revealed by silence and introspection.
- Abide by your innate acumen and wisdom to regroup and redirect as necessary.

The Spirit of Water is here to help you flow with the potency of your genius so you can fall into step with the great human enterprise to foster the welfare and happiness of all living beings, including the earth. This elemental Spirit is your quintessential conduit and ally in your journey closer to your sacred relevance and your stalwart messengers and guides.

- Explore various ancient practices and sacred teachings from around the world.
- Learn from many trustworthy spiritual teachers.
- Seek elders with sincere and trustworthy sagacity.
- Foster vital and dynamic relationships with your ancestors and invite their essential transmissions and support.
- Summon assistance from your animal spirit guides.
- Welcome visions in guided rituals, including rituals with sacred medicines and plants.

*The Spirit of Water inspires you
to embrace all creation
and her abundant and generous
resources, messengers,
and messages.*

KIDNEYS – BLADDER – REPRODUCTIVE ORGANS – BRAIN – SEA OF MARROW – EARS

SPIRIT OF WATER

Explosive Spiritual Disharmony

59

You may be mesmerized by a scarcity meta-narrative!

Damn, your innate wisdom may be capsized by the dominant scarcity narrative! The Spirit of Water acknowledges that you may be bamboozled by a maelstrom of distress, uncertainty, and disorientation in the dominant culture in your family, community, and/or nation. She signals that the sweeping collective reverence for financial security combined with the systemic fear of economic collapse may be skewing or stunting your development and growth. For instance, you may latch on to fiscal savings, mistaking them for your spiritual habitat, safety, and sustenance; or your relentless survival and scarcity "crisis" may turn your head away from your genius and rule out your sacred relevance, meaningful activity, and thoughtful productivity.

Either way, your sacred relevance is threatened—the self-serving meta-narrative created by economists, financial engineers, corporate predators, and politicians may have its claws in far enough. You are vulnerable to their self-interested, contrived, and biased commodification of human worth and consciously or unconsciously make yourself available to their disinformation.

- You may be disoriented or misled by the systemic and penetrating spiritual destabilization in the dominant culture or you contribute to it.
- You may be captivated and addicted to the intentional and opportunistic fearmongering of sensationalist media created by corporations to gain financially or you contribute to it.
- You may be falling for self-interested and inflamed rhetoric (and its reportage and dissemination) asserting the presence of pertinent and imminent danger or evil that justifies violence, attacks, economic sanctions endangering the well-being of living beings, and/or war or you contribute to it.

The Spirit of Water encourages you to shut out the loud and invasive sources of disinformation and indoctrination. She implores you to listen deep inside, long enough, to transcend the insidious and omnipresent fear-inducing narratives.

DISHARMONY STORY

You're on top of it. You live in a lovely house out on the periphery of a large city—your dream come true. You're close enough to enjoy the perks of culture and fine dining and far enough to get away from it all and snuggle up to your spouse and walk in the woods with your dog. More importantly, your mortgage is fully paid up, other debts are dwindling, your savings account is swelling, and your personal retirement plan is on track. You're safe and will be safe until you die.

You didn't get here by accident. The minute you graduated from high school, you leapt into the lucid and coherent world of accounting and spreadsheets. It was a no-brainer, it all comes down to debits and credits—the one and only voice of reason. You know what you're talking about, as you're the mastermind behind the production spreadsheets of an architectural firm. You have spent decades making sense out of creative chaos. These artist-types are crazy and if left to their own devices, they would mismanage and squander the company's resources to build their pie-in-the-sky concepts. However, thanks to your tight grip on the budget and astute planning, the projects, the company, and your job is viable long-term.

Basically, you have spreadsheets for everything. Back in the day when you had a condo, you were on the board and made sure you and the other owners weren't getting stiffed by contractors. When you renovated your house, you ran the show without a contractor—you'd rather keep track of the freelancers than get swindled by those scammers. And even then, you sourced all the materials to make sure you got the best deals. It was relentless. You also have to keep track of your spouse's expenses. Your head is in spreadsheets all day at work and you spend hours with them on the weekend too. You never know where you'd end up if it wasn't for your clever and watchful eye.

Whoa, hard way to live! The client is convinced their ship could go down any minute if their hyper-vigilance slips. In their world, there are unscrupulous wolves prowling around every corner threatening to destroy their security, whether it's their job or their home. While they claim they are safe, and spend most of their energy safe-guarding their financial security, their kidneys, adrenals, and sea of marrow speak of chronic fear, which often escalates to panic. To make matters worse, they're the first ones to get the coffee going at home and at the office and are the reliable source of an endless stream of sweet delicacies from a number of much-frequented and eulogized establishments. They've gone up in the world, as it used to be Timbits and Twinkies (actually, sometimes it still is).

Despite chronic anxiety and gripping fear, the client holds up a picture of their childhood and adolescence as idyllic: a big family, lots of love, lots of food, and the best Christmas parties ever. Yet upon closer inspection, the sessions reveal that their father worked excessively long hours in the construction business to hold on to a small house in an underprivileged neighbourhood with a bare-bones public school, and neither snow nor rain nor heat nor gloom of night prevented their mother from perfecting her chores. "They got us kids through high school and hockey and did the best they could," but despite some lean times, I see. "Oh yeah, we hit some hard times," they remember, "but we pulled together and got through."

Truth be told, it was tense and their father often lashed out. The boys had to step it up if they were going to become men worth their salt. They had to pull their weight around the house, play a mean hockey game, and stop doing all that arty stuff. "There's no point having your head in the clouds. Get back down here and get a move on. You've got real things to do, buddy." What's more, their artistic tendencies were ridiculed by their jock brothers, and the only way to gain their respect was to prove they could skate as fast as any of them and score just as many goals. Unfortunately, the bullying was not only a threat at home. My client was bullied as school and had to buff up to fight back and stay ahead of the pack.

Wherever they turned, endangerment and survival was the name of the game. They are traumatized by the bullying, financial uncertainty, and spiritual disorientation in their family; and they're swept up by the collective reverence for financial security combined with the systemic fear of economic collapse in the dominant culture. Hence, the client latches on to fiscal savings, mistaking them for their safety and sustenance. Unfortunately, their relentless survival and scarcity "crisis" turns their head away from their genius and obscures the discovery and manifestation of their sacred relevance, the most precious and secure abundance of all.

The Spirit of Water inspires you to honour Nature's invitation to go within, whether it's winter or not. She is summoning you into the roots of your Sacred Tree and encourages you to bask in the light of your sacred relevance. Listen for accessible guidance and follow the trail of insights that silence and introspection reveals.

KIDNEYS – BLADDER – REPRODUCTIVE ORGANS – BRAIN – SEA OF MARROW – EARS

SPIRIT OF WATER

Implosive Spiritual Disharmony

60

You may be engulfed by an external ethos deemed correct!

Uh-oh, you may absorb narratives that give away your power to a conventional world order. The Spirit of Water acknowledges that the possibility of shifting away from an external framework deemed authoritative, legitimate, or safe appears so impossible or frightening that you may not even perceive the possibility of acting on your own insights, dreams, or innate wisdom. Unfortunately, your conscious or unconscious subjugation to an ethos considered rightful or correct may rule out your sacred relevance, meaningful activity, and thoughtful productivity.

- You may believe that your safety and security is contingent on being tied down and/or dependent on the sanctity of a tradition, convention, institution, job, career, home, or relationship.
- You may persist in a profoundly frustrating, dissatisfying, or even threatening situation in your professional life, personal life, or both to remain in an ostensibly safe and secure haven.
- You may forgo your calling and surrender to the logic of an external world order and "truth" to belong and be lovable.
- You may succumb or consent to the inevitability and safety of marriage, heteronormative relationships, and/or procreation despite insights about your lack of passionate commitment to a particular individual or calling.
- You may be loyal, dutiful, and/or pious despite insights, private misgivings, suspicions, and/or substantiated proof of dishonesty, corruption, and/or exploitation of other living beings.

The Spirit of Water calls you back to your roots deep in the belly of the earth. Your truth and sacred relevance generate the safest wellspring of wisdom and mindful actions that you can rely on and act upon.

DISHARMONY STORY

Your father is your pillar of strength, willpower, and wisdom. He has shaped, informed, and orchestrated your world and your sense of where you belong since early on. You remember with such tenderness the carefree evenings and weekends when you played, danced, and skied together. He was also a big bundle of love and a sure bet for a light-hearted good time. You adore him so much and enjoy him more than anyone in the world, even his unrelenting goofy puns—you love it all. Besides, he rehabilitated eagles, he cared for all of his patients above and beyond the call of duty, he was respected by everyone in the community, and he even dedicated a lot of time and effort to help a young girl in your community who was sexually abused. He is your hero, and you were his golden princess.

However, by your mid-teens, you fear his disapproval constantly. You're anxious and distracted and not doing well in school. You just can't sit still long enough to absorb or retain information. Although you aspired to be an amazing doctor like him, you don't feel gifted enough academically and you're more drawn to the arts these days and want to be an actor. In addition, it's all falling apart on the homefront. You're constantly fighting with your mother, and both of you fly off the handle practically every time you're in the same room. Apparently, your "outrageous and self-centred" turmoil is wrecking it for everyone, and nothing you do is good enough for her gingerbread-perfect family. What's worse is that you see the clouds covering your dad's sun when your mom sways him with her perspective. What's more, you have your own shit going down and you know it would devastate him. You drink a lot, and once you're drunk who knows who you'll jump into bed with.

By your mid-twenties, you're even more outrageously outside princess territory. You're impulsive, you're a starving artist, and you're head over heels in love with a woman. If he knew the half of it, the paternal pillar would for sure be razed to the ground. Besides, it's getting worse by the day: you're actually cracking into a million lonely desperate pieces. The love of your life is abusing you (it seems like men don't have the copyright on that), and you're having more and more memories of being sexually abused by a family member you also adored.

It turns out the golden princess was a mere illusion in the gingerbread-household mythology way before the client "fucked up" in their teens. They are like that girl their father helped who was violated sexually, except for the part about being helped by their father. Their perfect father actually failed to witness that his beloved golden princess was being sexually abused right under his nose. He was so chuffed with his competence and drunk on the myth of his perfect career, wife, and children that the stench of reality didn't reach his nostrils in his own home.

60

His princess, the one who failed to be equal to the dream, actually suppressed their truth and sacrificed their Sacred Tree ecology on the altar of the gingerbread castle. The story of the castle and the story of their fall from grace often deafens their intuitive access to their innate wisdom and guidance still. On days when they feel shaky, they still succumb to the logic of that "perfect world order and truth" and yearn, despite the danger they were in, to belong to this ostensibly safe gingerbread haven. The compelling story of the perfect home and family is often more potent and believable to them than the telltale signs of their profound distress and the eruption of their horrifying truth into their day-to-day consciousness.

While the happy myth is still guarded with wet fangs by their mother and siblings and this flesh-and-blood child–teenager–adult remains isolated and vilified by them, their father is now a compassionate ancestor and guardian who witnesses, supports, and protects them unconditionally. He acknowledges their abuse and fully devotes himself to the well-being, growth, and emancipation of his daughter. He, more than anyone, actively recognizes their Sacred Tree and unconditionally loves and celebrates their magnificence, pain, rough edges, and all.

The Spirit of Water assures you that you are not alone with your truth! She is your conduit to your internal and external allies and guides. She encourages you to seek elders and spiritual teachers with sincere and trustworthy sagacity and to foster vital and dynamic relationships.

Dany Lyne uses the embodiment of high-frequency energy to activate full human potential. Her method ignites a new approach to living in creative genius and personal freedom through capturing and enhancing Loving Kindness and compassion in the four bodies: physical, emotional, mental, and spiritual. She draws from her experience as a trauma intuitive, Reiki practitioner, CranioSacral therapist, and studies with indigenous healers in Africa, Central America, and South America, insights during meditation, and her personal passion for stimulating her clients' connection to the life force. Her greatest joy is sharing her discoveries with others.

DANYLYNE.COM

Made in the USA
Middletown, DE
23 October 2023

41260316R00148